W9-BYW-162

interchange
FOURTH EDITION

Jack C. Richards
With Jonathan Hull and Susan Proctor

Series Editor: David Bohlke

CAMBRIDGE
UNIVERSITY PRESS

STUDENT'S BOOK

3

CAMBRIDGE
UNIVERSITY PRESS

32 Avenue of the Americas, New York, NY 10013-2473, USA

Cambridge University Press is part of the University of Cambridge.

It furthers the University's mission by disseminating knowledge in the pursuit of education, learning and research at the highest international levels of excellence.

www.cambridge.org
Information on this title: www.cambridge.org/9781107648708

© Cambridge University Press 2013

First published 1991
Second edition 1998
Third edition 2005
10th printing 2014

Printed in Mexico by Quad/ Graphics Queretaro, S.A. de C.V.

A catalog record for this publication is available from the British Library.

ISBN 978-1-107-64870-8 Student's Book 3 with Self-study DVD-ROM
ISBN 978-1-107-69720-1 Student's Book 3A with Self-study DVD-ROM
ISBN 978-1-107-65269-9 Student's Book 3B with Self-study DVD-ROM
ISBN 978-1-107-64874-6 Workbook 3
ISBN 978-1-107-64685-8 Workbook 3A
ISBN 978-1-107-68752-3 Workbook 3B
ISBN 978-1-107-61506-9 Teacher's Edition 3 with Assessment Audio CD/CD-ROM
ISBN 978-1-107-66870-6 Class Audio 3 CDs
ISBN 978-1-107-66684-9 Full Contact 3 with Self-study DVD-ROM
ISBN 978-1-107-62042-1 Full Contact 3A with Self-study DVD-ROM
ISBN 978-1-107-63667-5 Full Contact 3B with Self-study DVD-ROM

For a full list of components, visit www. cambridge.org/interchange

Art direction, book design, layout services, and photo research: Integra
Audio production: CityVox, NYC
Video production: Nesson Media Boston, Inc.

Welcome to *Interchange Fourth Edition*, the world's most successful English series!

Interchange offers a complete set of tools for learning how to communicate in English.

Student's Book
with NEW Self-study DVD-ROM

- **Complete video program** with additional **video exercises**

- Additional **vocabulary**, **grammar**, **speaking**, **listening**, and **reading** practice
- Printable **score reports** to submit to teachers

Available online

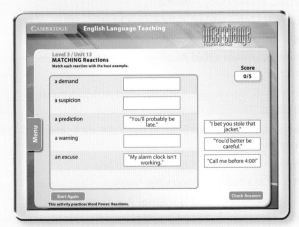

Interchange Arcade

- **Free** self-study website
- **Fun**, interactive, self-scoring activities
- Practice **vocabulary**, **grammar**, **listening**, and **reading**
- **MP3s** of the class audio program

Online Workbook

- A variety of **interactive activities** that correspond to each Student's Book lesson
- **Instant feedback** for hundreds of activities
- **Easy to use** with clear, easy-to-follow instructions
- Extra **listening practice**
- Simple tools for teachers to **monitor progress** such as scores, attendance, and time spent online

Authors' acknowledgments

A great number of people contributed to the development of *Interchange Fourth Edition*. Particular thanks are owed to the reviewers using *Interchange, Third Edition* in the following schools and institutes – their insights and suggestions have helped define the content and format of the fourth edition:

Ian Geoffrey Hanley, **The Address Education Center**, Izmir, Turkey

James McBride, **AUA Language Center**, Bangkok, Thailand

Jane Merivale, **Centennial College**, Toronto, Ontario, Canada

Elva Elena Peña Andrade, **Centro de Auto Aprendizaje de Idiomas**, Nuevo León, Mexico

José Paredes, **Centro de Educación Continua de la Escuela Politécnica Nacional** (CEC-EPN), Quito, Ecuador

Chia-jung Tsai, **Changhua University of Education**, Changhua City, Taiwan

Kevin Liang, **Chinese Culture University**, Taipei, Taiwan

Roger Alberto Neira Perez, **Colegio Santo Tomás de Aquino**, Bogotá, Colombia

Teachers at **Escuela Miguel F. Martínez**, Monterrey, Mexico

Maria Virgínia Goulart Borges de Lebron, **Great Idiomas**, São Paulo, Brazil

Gina Kim, **Hoseo University**, Chungnam, South Korea

Heeyong Kim, Seoul, South Korea

Elisa Borges, **IBEU-Rio**, Rio de Janeiro, Brazil

Jason M. Ham, **Inha University**, Incheon, South Korea

Rita de Cássia S. Silva Miranda, **Instituto Batista de Idiomas**, Belo Horizonte, Brazil

Teachers at **Instituto Politécnico Nacional**, Mexico City, Mexico

Victoria M. Roberts and Regina Marie Williams, **Interactive College of Technology**, Chamblee, Georgia, USA

Teachers at **Internacional de Idiomas**, Mexico City, Mexico

Marcelo Serafim Godinho, **Life Idiomas**, São Paulo, Brazil

J. Kevin Varden, **Meiji Gakuin University**, Yokohama, Japan

Rosa Maria Valencia Rodríguez, Mexico City, Mexico

Chung-Ju Fan, **National Kinmen Institute of Technology**, Kinmen, Taiwan

Shawn Beasom, **Nihon Daigaku**, Tokyo, Japan

Gregory Hadley, **Niigata University of International and Information Studies**, Niigata, Japan

Chris Ruddenklau, **Osaka University of Economics and Law**, Osaka, Japan

Byron Roberts, **Our Lady of Providence Girls' High School**, Xindian City, Taiwan

Simon Banha, **Phil Young's English School**, Curitiba, Brazil

Flávia Gonçalves Carneiro Braathen, **Real English Center**, Viçosa, Brazil

Márcia Cristina Barboza de Miranda, **SENAC**, Recife, Brazil

Raymond Stone, **Seneca College of Applied Arts and Technology**, Toronto, Ontario, Canada

Gen Murai, **Takushoku University**, Tokyo, Japan

Teachers at **Tecnológico de Estudios Superiores de Ecatepec**, Mexico City, Mexico

Teachers at **Universidad Autónoma Metropolitana–Azcapotzalco**, Mexico City, Mexico

Teachers at **Universidad Autónoma de Nuevo León**, Monterrey, Mexico

Mary Grace Killian Reyes, **Universidad Autónoma de Tamaulipas**, Tampico Tamaulipas, Mexico

Teachers at **Universidad Estatal del Valle de Ecatepec**, Mexico City, Mexico

Teachers at **Universidad Nacional Autónoma de Mexico – Zaragoza**, Mexico City, Mexico

Teachers at **Universidad Nacional Autónoma de Mexico – Iztacala**, Mexico City, Mexico

Luz Edith Herrera Diaz, Veracruz, Mexico

Seri Park, **YBM PLS**, Seoul, South Korea

Self-assessment charts revised by Alex Tilbury

Grammar plus written by Karen Davy

Plan of Book 3

Titles/Topics	Speaking	Grammar
UNIT 1 PAGES 2–7		
That's what friends are for! Personality types and qualities; relationships; turn ons and turn offs	Describing personalities; expressing likes and dislikes; agreeing and disagreeing; complaining	Relative pronouns as subjects and objects; *it* clauses + adverbial clauses with *when*
UNIT 2 PAGES 8–13		
Career moves Jobs; careers of the future; job skills; summer jobs	Talking about possible careers; describing jobs; discussing the negative aspects of some jobs	Gerund phrases as subjects and objects; comparisons with adjectives, nouns, verbs, and past participles
PROGRESS CHECK PAGES 14–15		
UNIT 3 PAGES 16–21		
Could you do me a favor? Favors; formal and informal requests; messages	Making unusual requests; making direct and indirect requests; accepting and declining requests	Requests with modals, *if* clauses, and gerunds; indirect requests
UNIT 4 PAGES 22–27		
What a story! The media; news stories; exceptional events	Narrating a story; describing events and experiences in the past	Past continuous vs. simple past; past perfect
PROGRESS CHECK PAGES 28–29		
UNIT 5 PAGES 30–35		
Crossing cultures Cultural comparisons and culture shock; moving abroad; emotions; customs; tourism and travel abroad	Talking about moving abroad; expressing emotions; describing cultural expectations; giving advice	Noun phrases containing relative clauses; expectations: *the custom to, (not) supposed to, expected to, (not) acceptable to*
UNIT 6 PAGES 36–41		
What's wrong with it? Consumer complaints; everyday problems; electronics; repairs	Describing problems; making complaints; explaining something that needs to be done	Describing problems with past participles as adjectives and with nouns; describing problems with *need* + gerund, *need* + passive infinitive, and *keep* + gerund
PROGRESS CHECK PAGES 42–43		
UNIT 7 PAGES 44–49		
The world we live in The environment; world problems; current issues	Identifying and describing problems; coming up with solutions	Passive in the present continuous and present perfect; prepositions of cause; infinitive clauses and phrases
UNIT 8 PAGES 50–55		
Lifelong learning Education; learner choices; strategies for learning; personal qualities	Asking about preferences; discussing pros and cons of different college majors; talking about learning methods; talking about personal qualities	*Would rather* and *would prefer; by* + gerund to describe how to do things
PROGRESS CHECK PAGES 56–57		

Pronunciation/Listening	Writing/Reading	Interchange Activity
Linked sounds Listening for descriptions of people; listening for opinions	Writing a description of a best friend "To Friend or Unfriend?": Reading about choosing online friends	"Personality types": Interviewing a classmate to find out about personality characteristics PAGE 114
Stress with compound nouns Listening to descriptions of summer jobs; listening for likes and dislikes	Writing about career advantages and disadvantages "Help! How Can I Find a Job?": Reading a message board with advice on how to find a job	"The dinner party": Comparing people's careers and personalities to make a seating chart for a dinner party PAGE 115
Unreleased consonants Listening to people making, accepting, and declining requests	Writing emails with requests "Yes or No?": Reading about the way people in different cultures respond "yes" and "no"	"Borrowers and lenders": Asking classmates to borrow items; lending or refusing to lend items PAGE 116
Intonation in complex sentences Listening to news podcasts; listening to narratives about past events	Writing a news story "The Changing World of Blogging": Reading about the evolution of blogs	"A double ending": Completing a story with two different endings PAGE 117
Word stress in sentences Listening for information about living abroad; listening to opinions about customs	Writing a tourist pamphlet "Culture Shock": Reading blog entries about moving to another country	"Culture check": Comparing customs in different countries PAGE 118
Contrastive stress Listening to complaints; listening to people exchange things in a store; listening to repair people describe their jobs	Writing a critical online review "The Value of Upcycling": Reading about reusing materials to make things of greater value	"Fixer-upper": Comparing problems in two pictures of an apartment PAGES 119, 120
Reduction of auxiliary verbs Listening to environmental problems; listening for solutions	Writing a message on a community website "Saving a Coral Reef – An Eco Tipping Point": Reading about reviving marine life around Apo Island	"Make your voices heard!": Choosing an issue and deciding on an effective method of protest; devising a strategy PAGE 121
Intonation in questions of choice Listening to descriptions of courses; listening for additional information	Writing about a skill or a hobby "Learning Styles": Reading about different kinds of learning	"Learning curves": Choosing between different things you want to learn PAGE 122

Titles/Topics	Speaking	Grammar
UNIT 9 PAGES 58–63		
Improvements Everyday services; recommendations; self-improvement	Talking about things you need to have done; asking for and giving advice or suggestions	Get or have something done; making suggestions with modals + verbs, gerunds, negative questions, and infinitives
UNIT 10 PAGES 64–69		
The past and the future Historic events and people; biography; the future	Talking about history events; talking about things to be accomplished in the future	Referring to time in the past with adverbs and prepositions: *during, in, ago, from…to, for, since*; predicting the future with *will*, future continuous, and future perfect
PROGRESS CHECK PAGES 70–71		
UNIT 11 PAGES 72–77		
Life's little lessons Milestones and turning points; behavior and personality; regrets	Describing rites of passage; describing turning points; describing regrets and hypothetical situations	Time clauses: *before, after, once, the moment, as soon as, until, by the time*; expressing regret with *should (not) have* + past participle; describing hypothetical situations with *if* clauses + past perfect
UNIT 12 PAGES 78–83		
The right stuff Qualities for success; successful businesses; advertising	Describing qualities for success; describing features; giving reasons for success; interviewing for a job; talking about ads and slogans	Describing purpose with infinitive clauses and infinitive clauses with *for*; giving reasons with *because, since, because of, for, due to*, and *the reason*
PROGRESS CHECK PAGES 84–85		
UNIT 13 PAGES 86–91		
That's a possibility. Pet peeves; unexplained events; reactions; complicated situations and advice	Making conclusions; offering explanations; describing hypothetical events; giving advice for complicated situations	Past modals for degrees of certainty: *must (not) have, may (not) have, might (not) have, could (not) have*; past modals for judgments and suggestions: *should (not) have, could (not) have, would (not) have*
UNIT 14 PAGES 92–97		
Behind the scenes How a movie is made; media professions; processes; the entertainment industry	Describing how something is done or made; describing careers in the media	The passive to describe process with *is/are* + past participle and modal + *be* + past participle; defining and non-defining relative clauses
PROGRESS CHECK PAGES 98–99		
UNIT 15 PAGES 100–105		
There should be a law! Recommendations; opinions; local concerns; controversial issues	Giving opinions for and against controversial issues; offering a different opinion; agreeing and disagreeing	Giving recommendations and opinions with passive modals: *should be, ought to be, must be, has to be, has got to be*; tag questions for opinions
UNIT 16 PAGES 106–111		
Challenges and accomplishments Challenges; accomplishments; goals; volunteering	Describing challenges, frustrations, and rewards; talking about the past and the future	Complex noun phrases containing gerunds; accomplishments with the present perfect and simple past; goals with the future perfect and *would like to have* + past participle
PROGRESS CHECK PAGES 112–113		
GRAMMAR PLUS PAGES 132–151		

Pronunciation/Listening	Writing/Reading	Interchange Activity
Sentence stress Listening to suggestions for self-improvement	Writing a letter of advice "Critical Thinking": Reading about the characteristics and benefits of critical thinking	"Put yourself in my shoes!": Discussing different points of view of parents and their children PAGE 123
Syllable stress Listening to predictions	Writing a biography "Tweet to Eat": Reading about a restaurant that uses social networking to reach customers	"History buff": Taking a history quiz PAGES 124, 126
Reduction of *have* and *been* Listening to descriptions of important events; listening to regrets and explanations	Writing a letter of apology "Milestones Around the World": Reading about important life events in Egypt, Mexico, and Vanuatu	"When I was younger,…": Playing a board game to talk about how you were and could have been PAGE 125
Reduced words Listening for features and slogans	Writing a radio or TV commercial "The Wrong Stuff": Reading about advertising failures	"Catchy slogans": Creating a slogan and logo for a product PAGE 127
Reduction in past modals Listening to explanations; listening for the best solution	Writing about a complicated situation "The Blue Lights of Silver Cliff": Reading a story about an unexplained phenomenon	"Photo plays": Drawing possible conclusions about situations PAGE 128
Review of stress in compound nouns Listening to a producer describe his work; listening for personality traits	Writing about a process "Hooray for Bollywood!": Reading about the kind of movies made in India	"Who makes it happen?": Putting together a crew for making a movie PAGE 129
Intonation in tag questions Listening for solutions to everyday annoyances; listening to issues and opinions	Writing a persuasive essay "How Serious Is Plagiarism?": Reading about plagiarism and people's opinions about its severity	"You be the judge!": Deciding on punishments for common offenses PAGE 130
Stress and rhythm Listening to challenges and rewards of people's work; listening for people's goals for the future	Writing a personal statement for an application "Young and Gifted": Reading about exceptionally gifted young people	"Viewpoints": Taking a survey about volunteering PAGE 131

That's what friends are for!

1 SNAPSHOT

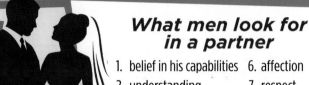

Love and Marriage in North America

What women look for in a partner

1. love
2. understanding
3. conversation
4. time together
5. a positive attitude
6. a good listener
7. affection
8. responsibility at home
9. free time
10. good health

What men look for in a partner

1. belief in his capabilities
2. understanding
3. compliments
4. acceptance
5. direct conversation
6. affection
7. respect
8. free time
9. trust
10. companionship

Source: http://marriage.about.com

What qualities do both men and women look for in their partners?
In your opinion, which of the things above are most important to look for in a partner?
Are there other important qualities missing from the lists?

2 CONVERSATION *I like guys who . . .*

A ▶ Listen and practice.

Chris: Do you have a date for your friend's wedding yet?

Kim: Actually, no, I don't. . . . Do you know anyone I could go with?

Chris: Hmm. What kind of guys do you like?

Kim: Oh, I like guys who aren't too serious and who have a good sense of humor. You know, someone like you.

Chris: OK. Uh, what else?

Kim: Well, I'd prefer someone I have something in common with – who I can talk to easily.

Chris: I think I know just the guy for you. Bob Branson. Do you know him?

Kim: No, I don't think so.

Chris: OK, I'll ask him to meet us for coffee, and you can tell me what you think.

B ▶ Listen to Chris and Kim discuss Bob after they met for coffee. How did Kim like him?

3 GRAMMAR FOCUS

Relative pronouns ▶

As the subject of a clause
I like guys **who/that** aren't too serious.
I like guys **who/that** have a good sense of humor.

As the object of a clause
I'd prefer someone **(who/that)** I have fun with.
I'd prefer someone **(who/that)** I can talk to easily.

A Match the information in columns A and B. Then compare with a partner.

A

1. I don't want to have a partner who/that ....d....
2. I enjoy teachers who/that ....a....
3. I'd prefer a roommate who/that ....g....
4. I don't like to be with people who/that ....f....
5. I discuss my problems with friends who/that ....e....
6. I'd like to have a boss who/that ....b....
7. I like to meet people who/that ....c....

B

a. help me understand things easily.
b. I respect as a leader.
c. have a good sense of humor.
d. I have nothing in common with.
e. can give me good advice.
f. I don't feel comfortable around.
g. is quiet, considerate, and neat.

B Put a line through *who/that* in part A if it's optional. Then compare with a partner.

C PAIR WORK Complete the sentences in column A with your own information.
Do you and your partner have similar opinions?

A: I don't want to have a partner who isn't a good listener.
B: Neither do I. I don't want to have a partner who doesn't have a positive attitude either.

4 WORD POWER Personalities

A Match the words with the definitions. Then decide whether the words are
positive (**P**) or negative (**N**). Write **P** or **N** after each word.

....h.... 1. easygoing ....P....
....c.... 2. egotistical ....N....
....a.... 3. inflexible ....N....
....i.... 4. modest ....P....
....f.... 5. sociable ....P....
....b.... 6. stingy ....N....
....d.... 7. supportive ....P....
....g.... 8. temperamental ....N....
....e.... 9. unreliable ....N....

a. a person who doesn't change easily and is stubborn
b. someone who doesn't like sharing
c. someone who has a very high opinion of him- or herself
d. someone who is helpful and encouraging
e. a person who doesn't do what he or she promised
f. a person who enjoys being with other people
g. a person who has unpredictable or irregular moods
h. a person who doesn't worry much or get angry easily
i. someone who doesn't brag about his or her accomplishments

B PAIR WORK Cover the definitions. Take turns talking about the adjectives in your own words.

"An easygoing person is someone who . . ."

C PAIR WORK Think of at least two adjectives to describe yourself. Then tell a partner.

5 LISTENING *What are they like?*

A ▶ Listen to conversations that describe three people. Are the descriptions positive (**P**) or negative (**N**)? Check (✓) the box.

1. Andrea ☐ P ☐ N ....
2. James ☑ P ☐ N ....
3. Mr. Johnson ☐ P ☐ N ....

B ▶ Listen again. Write two adjectives that describe each person in the chart.

6 DISCUSSION *Ideal people*

A What is the ideal parent, friend, or partner like? What is one quality each should have and one quality each should *not* have? Complete the chart.

	This person is . . .	This person is not . . .
The ideal parent	is supportitive	is not unriliable
The ideal friend	is easygoing	is not temperamental
The ideal partner	is sociable	is not egotistical

B GROUP WORK Take turns describing your ideal people. Try to agree on the two most important qualities for a parent, a friend, and a partner.

A: I think the ideal parent is someone who is easygoing and who . . .
B: I agree. The ideal parent is someone that doesn't get upset easily and who isn't temperamental.
C: Oh, I'm not sure I agree. . . .

7 WRITING *About a best friend*

A Think about your best friend. Answer the questions. Then write a paragraph.

What is your best friend like?
How long have you been friends?
How did you meet?
How are you similar?
How are you different?

> My best friend is someone who (that) is friendly and easygoing. She's a reliable friend and someone who I can call anytime. We've been friends for about five years, but we didn't become friends right away. We . . .

B PAIR WORK Exchange paragraphs. How are your best friends similar? How are they different?

A ▶ Listen to some common complaints. Check (✓) the ones you agree with.

Do you get annoyed easily?

- [✓] I can't stand it when a child screams in a restaurant.
- [ ] I don't like it when a cell phone rings in the classroom.
- [ ] It bothers me when a teacher forgets my name.
- [✓] I hate it when people talk with their mouths full.
- [✓] It upsets me when a close friend forgets my birthday.
- [✓] I can't stand it when people talk loudly to each other during a movie.
- [ ] I don't like it when people call me early in the morning.
- [✓] It bothers me when my doctor arrives late for an appointment.

Score: If you checked . . .
1–2 complaints: Wow! You don't get annoyed very easily.
3–4 complaints: You're fairly easygoing.
5–6 complaints: You get annoyed pretty easily.
7–8 complaints: Relax! You get annoyed too easily.

B Calculate your score. Do you get annoyed easily? Tell the class what bothers you the most.

9 **PRONUNCIATION** Linked sounds

A ▶ Listen and practice. Final consonant sounds are often linked to the vowel sounds that follow them.

It upsets me when a person is unreliable.

I love it when a friend is supportive and kind.

B ▶ Mark the linked sounds in the sentences below. Listen and check. Then practice saying the sentences.

1. I can't stand it when someone is late for an appointment.

2. Does it bother you when a friend is unreliable?

3. I hate it when a cell phone goes off in class.

C Take turns saying the sentences in Exercise 8. Pay attention to linked sounds.

It *clauses* + adverbial *clauses* with *when* ▶

I like **it**	— **when** a teacher is helpful and supportive.
I don't mind **it**	**when** a friend visits without calling me first.
I can't stand **it**	**when** a child screams in a restaurant.
It makes me happy	**when** people do nice things for no reason.
It bothers me	**when** my doctor arrives late for an appointment.
It upsets me	**when** a close friend forgets my birthday.

A How do you feel about these situations? Complete the sentences with *it* clauses from the list. Then take turns reading your sentences with a partner.

[handwritten: it's ok   not good thing → annoys]

I love it	I don't mind it	I don't like it
I like it	It doesn't bother me	It really upsets me
It makes me happy	It annoys me	I can't stand it

1. _I dont mind it_ when someone gives me a compliment.
2. _I love it_ when I get phone calls on my birthday.
3. _I don't like it_ when a stranger asks me for money.
4. _It doesnt bother me_ when people call me late at night.
5. _I can't stand it_ when teachers are temperamental.
6. _I like it_ when people are direct and say what's on their mind.
7. _It annoys me_ when someone corrects my English in front of others.
8. _I like it_ when a friend is sensitive and supportive.
9. _It really upsets me_ when people throw trash on the ground.
10. _It makes me happy_ when a friend treats me to dinner.

B GROUP WORK Do you ever get annoyed by a certain type of person or situation? Write down five things that annoy you the most. Then compare in groups.

A: I can't stand it when someone puts me on hold.
B: I feel the same way.
C: Yeah, but it bothers me more when . . .

11 INTERCHANGE 1 *Personality types*

Interview a classmate to find out about his or her personality.
Go to Interchange 1 on page 114.

To Friend or Unfriend?

How do you choose your friends online?
What qualities do you look for in cyberfriends?

Social networking makes it very easy to have friends – lots and lots of friends. Hundreds of millions of people have joined Facebook, Orkut, and other sites so that they can communicate with their friends online. However, the meaning of the word "friend" seems to have changed. In the past, a friend was someone you had a close personal relationship with. Now, anyone in the world can be your friend online! Some people have thousands of cyberfriends, but what do you do if you don't want so many friends?

Easy! You can dump an unwanted friend with just one click of your mouse. In recent years, it has become so common to get rid of friends in this way that there is a new word to describe it – to "unfriend." The *New Oxford American Dictionary* named it Word of the Year in 2009 and defined it like this: "to remove someone as a 'friend' from a social networking site." But why would you want to do such a drastic thing as unfriend someone?

The most common reason for unfriending someone is to eliminate annoying people from your social life. For example, some friends post messages much too frequently – and those messages can be extremely boring. They endlessly post status updates that say things like "I'm cooking dinner" or "I'm doing my homework." Another reason for unfriending someone is disagreement about world issues. A third reason is to get rid of people who write nasty things on social websites.

Although dumping friends is not just an Internet phenomenon, far more online friendships end suddenly than off-line ones. Even in this computer age, it remains true that many people prefer spending time together face-to-face. After all, that's what friends are for!

A Read the article. Then for each statement, check (✓) True, False, or Not given.

	True	False	Not given
1. Social networking has changed the way many people make friends.	✓		
2. It's not easy to remove cyberfriends.		✓	
3. The word "unfriend" became popular in 2009.	✓		
4. People who are unfriended may feel upset.			✓
5. Some people write unpleasant things on websites.	✓		
6. Sometimes family members are unfriended from websites.			✓

B Find the words and phrases in *italics* in the text. Then choose the meaning for each one.

1. When you have a *personal relationship*, you **know** / **don't know** someone well.
2. If you *dump* people you know, you **friend** / **unfriend** them.
3. You might do something *drastic* when you feel **easygoing** / **strongly** about it.
4. When you *eliminate* someone from your life, you **add** / **remove** them.
5. If you are *face-to-face* with someone, you are in **the same** / **a different** location.

C **PAIR WORK** Have you ever unfriended anyone? Why? Have you ever been unfriended? How did you feel?

2 Career moves

HOT JOBS ▸ *In-demand careers of the future* ▸

☐ **Simulation engineer** You develop different kinds of simulators, such as flight simulators for training pilots or virtual patients for training medical students.

☐ **Health informatics technician** You use computer systems to update patients' files, which helps doctors diagnose and treat patients.

☐ **Green researcher** You research new environmentally friendly technologies for fields such as transportation, energy, and recycling.

☐ **Organic food farmer** You grow healthy food in a sustainable way, without using harmful pesticides or chemicals.

☐ **Social media manager** You control the representation of a company's brand online on sites like Facebook, Twitter, and others.

Source: www.careerbuilder.com

Rank the careers from 1 (most interesting) to 5 (least interesting). Compare with a partner.
Can you think of any other careers that will be in demand in the future?
What jobs do you think will not be in demand? Why?

2 PERSPECTIVES *Career debate*

A ◉ Listen to the people talk about jobs. Do you agree or disagree?
Check (✓) the speaker you agree with more.

"Being a flight attendant sounds very exciting. Flying all the time would be fun."
☐

"But flight attendants get tired of traveling. They spend most of their time in airports!"
☐

"Designing clothes is not a man's job. Women are much more fascinated by fashion."
☐

"That's not true! Many great clothing designers are men. Just look at Calvin Klein!"
☐

"I'd enjoy working with animals. I think working as a veterinarian could be rewarding."
☐

"I'm not so sure. Animals can be very unpredictable. Getting a dog bite would be scary!"
☐

"I'd like to work in the television industry. Directing a TV show would be really interesting."
☐

"I disagree! Working in front of the camera as an actor would be much more satisfying."
☐

B Compare your responses with your classmates. Give more reasons to support your opinions.

Gerund phrases ▶

Gerund phrases as subjects
Being a flight attendant sounds exciting.
Designing clothes is not a man's job.
Working as a veterinarian could be rewarding.
Directing a TV show would be interesting.

Gerund phrases as objects
He'd love **being a flight attendant**.
He wouldn't like **being a fashion designer**.
She'd enjoy **working with animals**.
She'd be good at **directing a TV show**.

A Look at the gerund phrases in column A. Write your opinion of each job by choosing information from columns B and C. Then add two more gerund phrases and write similar sentences.

A	B	C
1. working as an accountant	seems	awful
2. taking care of children	sounds	stressful
3. being a farmer	could be	fantastic
4. designing clothes	would be	fascinating
5. working on a movie set	must be	pretty difficult
6. making a living as an artist		kind of boring
7. doing volunteer work overseas		really rewarding
8. retiring at age 40		very challenging
9.		
10.		

1. Working as an accountant would be kind of boring.

B **PAIR WORK** Give reasons for your opinions about the jobs in part A.

A: In my opinion, working as an accountant would be kind of boring.
B: Really? Why is that?
A: Because you work in an office and do the same thing every day.
B: I'm not sure that's true. For me, working as an accountant could be . . .

C **GROUP WORK** Complete the sentences with gerund phrases. Then take turns reading your sentences. Share the three most interesting sentences with the class.

1. I'd be interested in . . .
2. I'd get tired of . . .
3. I'd be very excited about . . .
4. I'd enjoy . . .
5. I think I'd be good at . . .
6. I wouldn't be very good at . . .

"I'd be interested in working with children."

4 WORD POWER *Suffixes*

A Add the suffixes *-er, -or, -ist*, or *-ian* to form the names of these jobs.
Write the words in the chart and add one more example to each column.

computer technic..<u>ian</u>...   gossip column............   politic............   TV report............
factory supervis............   guidance counsel............   psychiatr............   zookeep............

-er	-or	-ist	-ian
			computer technician

B PAIR WORK Can you give a definition for each job?

"A computer technician is someone who fixes computers."

5 SPEAKING *Possible careers*

GROUP WORK Talk about a career you would
like to have. Use information from Exercises 1–4 or your
own ideas. Other students ask follow-up questions.

A: I'd enjoy doing TV interviews with famous people.
B: Why is that?
A: Asking people about their lives would be fascinating.
C: Who would you interview?
A: Well, I think I'd be good at talking to politicians.

6 WRITING *Describing pros and cons*

A Choose a job and make a list of its advantages. Then use the list to
write a paragraph about the job. Add a title.

> <u>Being a comedian: It's fun to be funny</u>
> Working as a comedian seems exciting.
> First of all, making people laugh would be a
> lot of fun because you'd be laughing all the
> time, too. In addition, . . .

useful expressions
First of all, . . .
In addition, . . .
Furthermore, . . .
For example, . . .
However, . . .
On the other hand, . . .
In conclusion, . . .

B PAIR WORK Read your partner's paragraph. Then write a paragraph
about the disadvantages of your partner's job. Add a title.

C PAIR WORK Read your partner's paragraph about your job's
disadvantages. Do you agree or disagree? Why or why not?

7 CONVERSATION *You get a great tan!*

A ▶ Listen and practice.

Tracy: Guess what. . . . I've found a summer job!
Mark: That's great! Anything interesting?
Tracy: Yes, working at an amusement park.
Mark: Wow, that sounds fantastic!
Tracy: So, have *you* found anything?
Mark: Nothing yet, but I have a couple of leads. One is working as an intern for a record company – mostly answering phones. Or I can get a landscaping job again.
Tracy: Being an intern sounds more interesting than landscaping. You'd have better hours, and it's probably not as much work.
Mark: Yeah, but a landscaper earns more than an intern. And you get a great tan!

B ▶ Listen to the rest of the conversation. What is Tracy going to do at the amusement park?

8 GRAMMAR FOCUS

Comparisons ▶

with adjectives
. . . is **more/less** interesting **than** . . .
. . . is hard**er than** . . .
. . . is **not as** hard **as** . . .

with verbs
. . . earns **more/less than** . . .
. . . earns **as much as** . . .
. . . does**n't** earn **as much as** . . .

with nouns
. . . has **better/worse** hours **than** . . .
. . . has **more** education **than** . . .
. . . is**n't as much** work **as** . . .

with past participles
. . . is **better** paid **than** . . .
. . . is **as** well paid **as** . . .
. . . is**n't as** well paid **as** . . .

A Complete the sentences using the words in parentheses. Compare with a partner. (More than one answer is possible.)

1. Being a fashion designer is .... (interesting) being an accountant.
2. A TV reporter's job is .... (dangerous) a firefighter's job.
3. A police officer .... (travel) a flight attendant.
4. A factory supervisor .... (earn) a volunteer teacher.
5. Long-distance truck drivers have .... (hours) bank tellers.
6. Pilots usually have .... (education) airport security guards.
7. A doctor is .... (trained) a medical assistant.
8. A social worker isn't .... (paid) a pharmacist.

B GROUP WORK Make one more comparison for each pair of jobs in part A.

Career moves ▪ 11

9 PRONUNCIATION *Stress with compound nouns*

A ▶ Listen and practice. Notice that the first word in these compound nouns has more stress. Then add two more compound nouns to the chart.

●	●	●	●
zookeeper firefighter	bank teller truck driver	gossip columnist guidance counselor	....

B GROUP WORK Which job in each column would be more interesting? Why? Tell the group. Pay attention to stress.

10 LISTENING *Summer jobs*

A ▶ Listen to three people talk about their summer jobs. Number the pictures from 1 to 3.

B ▶ Listen again. Do they like their jobs? Why or why not?

11 ROLE PLAY *My job is the worst!*

A Choose a job from the unit. Make a list of all the reasons why you *wouldn't* like it. Think about what is negative, difficult, or boring about it – the salary, the hours, the location, etc.

B GROUP WORK Role-play a discussion. Explain why your job is the worst!

A: I'm a teacher, and my salary is terrible!
B: I'm a doctor. I have a higher salary than a teacher, but a teacher has better hours.
C: Well, I'm a taxi driver. My hours aren't as bad as a doctor's, but . . .

12 INTERCHANGE 2 *The dinner party*

Would you be a good party planner? Go to Interchange 2 on page 115.

13 READING

Help! How can I find a job?

Make a short list of things people should do to find a job. Then scan the message board. Has riley18 done any of these things?

I've been job-hunting for a year with no luck. I've done all the right things. I graduated with a degree in information technology – everybody says you can't go wrong with IT! I've sent my résumé to lots of local companies. I dress professionally and answer interview questions well. But I haven't gotten a single job offer! Other applicants have work experience. How can I get experience if no one offers me a job? Help!
riley18

What kinds of jobs are you applying for? I figure you're aiming too high. Don't be too proud! Entering the job market for the first time requires you to be modest. Good luck!
erikjones

The thing about IT is you need to specialize. I work in medicine. Diagnostic imaging – stuff like PET and MRI scanning – uses complex software that can only be operated by highly specialized people.
maggie_ks

I had the same problem as you. I graduated in IT, too! Then I went to a career counselor. She made me realize I'm more suited to a job with people than one with computers. I'm a really sociable person. I applied for work in telesales and got a job immediately. I love it! I talk to people on the phone all day!
jackie_s

Don't just sit there and expect a job to come to you! When job-hunting, the three most important things to remember are location, location, location! Hit the streets and go where the jobs are!
luis005

There are so many more interesting jobs than working with computers! Why does everyone think IT is so special? Everyone has to eat and drink! Why don't you open a coffee shop or restaurant?
table9_5

A Read the message board. Where do these sentences belong?
Write the username of the person who probably made each comment.

_maggie_ks_ 1. Do something that others can't do!
.... 2. The key thing is to get a job and then work your way up.
.... 3. If you're prepared to relocate, you'll easily find a job in IT.
.... 4. Have you thought about being self-employed?
.... 5. Working alone all day on a computer isn't much fun for me!

B Whose advice would riley18 *most* likely follow in each of these situations?
Write the username.

.... 1. if he can move to a new place easily
.... 2. if he is happy to seek professional advice
.... 3. if he is prepared to study for another degree
.... 4. if he has some money to invest in a small business
.... 5. if he is patient enough to wait for promotion

C **GROUP WORK** Whose comment do you think is the most helpful to riley18? Why?
What advice or comment would you offer?

Units 1–2 Progress check

SELF-ASSESSMENT

How well can you do these things? Check (✓) the boxes.

I can	Very well	OK	A little
Describe personalities (Ex. 1)	☐	☐	☐
Ask about and express preferences (Ex. 1)	☐	☐	☐
Understand and express complaints (Ex. 2)	☐	☐	☐
Give opinions about jobs (Ex. 3)	☐	☐	☐
Describe and compare different jobs (Ex. 4)	☐	☐	☐

1 SPEAKING People preferences

A What two qualities would you like someone to have for these situations?

A person to ...
1. go on vacation with   ....
2. share an apartment with   ....
3. work on a class project with   ....

B CLASS ACTIVITY Find someone you could do each thing with.

A: What kind of person would you like to go on vacation with?
B: I'd prefer someone who is fairly independent.
A: Me, too! And I like to travel with someone who I can . . .

2 LISTENING Our biggest complaints

A Listen to Ann and John discuss these topics. Complete the chart.

	John's biggest complaint	Ann's biggest complaint
1. taxi drivers	....	....
2. people with dogs	....	....
3. TV commercials	....	....
4. store clerks	....	....

B PAIR WORK What is your biggest complaint about the topics in part A?

"I can't stand it when taxi drivers don't have change. . . ."

3 SURVEY *Good and bad points*

A **GROUP WORK** What job would you like to have? Ask and answer questions in groups to complete the chart.

Name	Job	Good points	Bad points
1.	....	....	....
2.	....	....	....
3.	....	....	....
4.	....	....	....

A: What job would you like to have?
B: I'd like to be a chef.
C: What would be the good points?
B: Well, thinking of menus would be fun.
D: Would there be any bad points?
B: Oh, sure. I'd dislike working long hours. . . .

useful expressions

I would(n't) be good at . . .
I would enjoy/dislike . . .
I would(n't) be interested in . . .
I would(n't) be excited about . . .

B **GROUP WORK** Who thought of the most unusual job? the best job? the worst job?

4 ROLE PLAY *Job headhunter*

Student A: Imagine you're a headhunter. You find jobs for people. Based on Student B's opinions about jobs in Exercise 3, offer two other jobs that Student B might enjoy.

Student B: Imagine you are looking for a job. Student A suggests two jobs for you. Discuss the questions below. Then choose one of the jobs.

Which one is more interesting? harder?
Which one has better hours? better pay?
Which job would you rather have?

A: I have two jobs for you. You could be a high school basketball coach or a veterinarian.
B: Hmm. Which job is more interesting?
A: Well, a veterinarian's job is more interesting than a job as a basketball coach, but . . .

Change roles and try the role play again.

WHAT'S NEXT?

Look at your Self-assessment again. Do you need to review anything?

3 Could you do me a favor?

1 SNAPSHOT

Favors People Dislike Being Asked

Could you...?

- buy me a coffee
- treat me to a movie
- fix my computer
- babysit my kids
- lend me some money
- help me move to a new apartment
- pick up some groceries
- donate to my favorite charity

Source: http://answers.yahoo.com

Imagine that a close friend asked you each of these favors. Which would you agree to do?
What are three other favors that you dislike being asked?

2 CONVERSATION *Would you mind...?*

A ▶ Listen and practice.

Min-gu: Hello?
  Jana: Hi, Min-gu. This is Jana.
Min-gu: Oh, hi, Jana. What's up?
  Jana: My best friend is in a band, and I'm going to one of his concerts this weekend. I'd love to take some pictures for his website. Would you mind if I borrowed your new camera?
Min-gu: Um, no. That's OK, I guess. I don't think I'll need it for anything.
  Jana: Thanks a million.
Min-gu: Sure. Uh, have you used a camera like mine before? It's sort of complicated.
  Jana: Uh-huh, sure, a couple of times. Would it be OK if I picked it up on Friday night?
Min-gu: Yeah, I guess so.

B ▶ Listen to two more calls Jana makes. What else does she want to borrow? Do her friends agree?

Requests with modals, if clauses, and gerunds ▶

Less formal

↓

More formal

Can I borrow your pen, please?
Could you lend me a jacket, please?
Is it OK if I use your phone?
Do you mind if I use your laptop for a minute?
Would it be all right if I compar**ed** our homework?
Would you mind if I borrow**ed** your new camera?
Would you mind babysitt**ing** my kids on Saturday night?
I was wondering if I **could** borrow some money.

A Circle the correct answers. Then practice with a partner.

1. A: Would you mind **help** / **helped** / **helping** me paint on Saturday?
   B: No, I don't mind. I'm not doing anything then.

2. A: I was wondering **I could** / **if I could** / **if I would** borrow your gold earrings.
   B: Sure, that's fine. Just don't lose them!

3. A: **Is it OK if** / **Would** / **Do you mind** I use your cell phone?
   B: No problem, but can you keep it short?

4. A: Would you mind if I **use** / **using** / **used** your car to pick up some groceries?
   B: Sorry, but it's not working. It's at the mechanic's.

5. A: Could you **lend** / **lending** / **lent** me your suit for a wedding?
   B: Of course. But you should dry-clean it first.

6. A: **Would you mind** / **Can** / **Is it OK if** you buy me a snack from the vending machine, please?
   B: Sorry, I don't have any change.

B Rewrite these sentences to make them more formal requests. Then practice making your requests with a partner. Accept or decline each request.

1. Lend me some money for a soda.
2. Return these books to the library for me.
3. Let me borrow your math homework.
4. I'd like to borrow your cell phone to call my friend in London.
5. Can I look at that magazine when you've finished reading it?
6. Help me clean the house before Mom and Dad get home.

1. Would you mind lending me some money for a soda?

Could you do me a favor? ▪ **17**

4 PRONUNCIATION *Unreleased consonants*

A ▶ Listen and practice. Notice that when /t/, /d/, /k/, /g/, /p/, and /b/ are followed by other consonant sounds, they are unreleased.

Coul**d D**oug ta**ke** care of my pe**t** spider?
Can you as**k** Bo**b** to hel**p** me?

B ▶ Circle the unreleased consonants in the conversations. Listen and check. Then practice the conversations with a partner.

1. A: I was wondering if I could borrow that book.
   B: Yes, but can you take it back to Greg tomorrow?

2. A: Would you mind giving Albert some help moving that big bed?
   B: Sorry, but my doctor said my back needs rest.

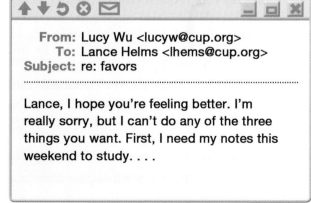

5 LISTENING *Favors*

A ▶ Listen to three telephone conversations. Write down what each caller requests. Does the other person agree to the request? Check (✓) Yes or No.

Request	Yes	No
1. Tina	☐	☐
2. Kyle	☐	☐
3. Phil	☐	☐

B **PAIR WORK** Use the chart to act out each conversation in your own words.

6 WRITING *An email request*

A Write an email to a classmate asking for several favors. Explain why you need help.

B **PAIR WORK** Exchange emails. Write a reply accepting or declining the requests.

From: Lance Helms <lhems@cup.org>
To: Lucy Wu <lucyw@cup.org>
Subject: favors

Lucy, I really need a few small favors. I hope you don't mind! I had a terrible cold last week, and I missed a couple of classes. I was wondering if I could borrow your notes. Also, . . .

From: Lucy Wu <lucyw@cup.org>
To: Lance Helms <lhems@cup.org>
Subject: re: favors

Lance, I hope you're feeling better. I'm really sorry, but I can't do any of the three things you want. First, I need my notes this weekend to study. . . .

7 INTERCHANGE 3 Borrowers and lenders

Find out how generous you are. Go to Interchange 3 on page 116.

8 WORD POWER Collocations

A Which verb is *not* usually paired with each noun? Put a line through the verb. Then compare with a partner.

1. (do / receive / give / accept)   a gift
2. (owe / offer / do / accept)   an apology
3. (do / return / make / receive)   a phone call
4. (return / do / ask for / make)   a favor
5. (receive / accept / turn down / offer) an invitation
6. (accept / make / decline / offer)   a request
7. (receive / return / do / give)   a compliment

B **PAIR WORK** Add two questions to the list using the collocations in part A. Then take turns asking and answering the questions.

1. When was the last time you received a gift from someone? What was it?
2. Have you ever *not* accepted someone's apology? Why not?
3. Do you usually return phone calls that you miss? Why or why not?
4. ....
5. ....

9 PERSPECTIVES Could you tell Jeff ...?

A Listen to the messages Jeff's assistant received while Jeff was away at lunch today. Complete each request with *ask* or *tell*.

1. Could you .... Jeff that Tony is having a party on Friday night?

2. Could you .... Jeff what he would like me to get him for his birthday?

3. Jeff is picking me up after basketball practice. Can you .... him not to be late?

4. Please .... Jeff that I owe him an apology – I forgot about our date last night.

5. Can you .... Jeff to return my call? I need to know when his report will be ready.

6. Could you .... Jeff whether he can come to class on Friday night instead of Thursday?

B Who do you think left each message?

his boss   his friend   his girlfriend   his mother   his teacher   his younger sister

Indirect requests ▶

Statements	Indirect requests introduced by *that*
Jeff, Tony is having a party. →	Could you tell Jeff **(that) Tony is having a party**?

Imperatives	Indirect requests using infinitives
Jeff, don't be late. →	Can you tell Jeff **not to be late**?

Yes/No questions	Indirect requests introduced by *if* or *whether*
Sofia, are you free on Friday? →	Can you ask Sofia **if she's free on Friday**?
Sofia, do you have my number? →	Could you ask her **whether or not she has my number**?

Wh-questions	Indirect requests introduced by a question word
Jeff, when does the party start? →	Can you ask Jeff **when the party starts**?
Sofia, what time should I pick you up? →	Could you ask Sofia **what time I should pick her up**?

Rewrite these sentences as indirect requests. In other words, ask someone to deliver the message for you. Then compare with a partner.

1. Nina, will you drive us to the party on Friday?
2. Tony, how many friends can I bring to your party?
3. Sofia, are you going to the party with Jeff?
4. Kevin, did you accept the invitation to Tony's party?
5. Mario, are you going to give Tony a gift?
6. Anne-Marie, please return my phone call.
7. Dan, where is the best place to park?
8. Kimberly, I have to turn down your invitation to the movies.

> 1. Could you ask Nina if she'll drive us to the party on Friday?

 SPEAKING *Pass it on.*

A Write five unusual requests for your partner to pass on to classmates.

> Would you ask Jin-sook if she could lend me $100?

B CLASS ACTIVITY Ask your partner to pass on your requests. Go around the class and make your partner's requests. Then tell your partner how people responded.

A: Would you ask Jin-sook if she could lend me $100?
B: Sure. . . . Jin-sook, could you lend Isam $100?
C: I'm sorry, but I can't! Could you tell Isam I'm broke?
B: Isam, Jin-sook says that she's broke.

YES or NO?

Scan the article. Where did the three events occur?

1 Living in a foreign culture can be exciting, but it can also be confusing. A group of Americans who taught English in other countries recently discussed their experiences. They decided that miscommunications were always possible, even over something as simple as "yes" and "no."

2 On her first day in Micronesia, Lisa thought people were ignoring her requests. The day was hot, and she needed a cold drink. She went into a store and asked, "Do you have cold drinks?" The woman there didn't say anything. Lisa rephrased the question. Still the woman said nothing. Lisa gave up and left the store. She later learned that the woman had answered her: She had raised her eyebrows, which in Micronesia means "yes."

3 This reminded Jan of an experience she had in Bulgaria. She had gone to a restaurant that was known for its stuffed cabbage. She asked the waiter, "Do you have stuffed cabbage today?" He nodded his head. Jan eagerly waited, but the cabbage never came. In that country, a nod means "no."

4 Tom had a similar problem when he arrived in India. After explaining something in class, he asked his students if they understood. They responded with many different nods and shakes of the head. He assumed some people had not understood, so he explained again. When he asked again if they understood, they did the same thing. He soon found out that his students did understand. In India, people nod and shake their heads in different ways depending on where they come from. You have to know where a person is from to understand if they are indicating "yes" or "no."

A Read the article. Then answer the questions.

1. What were these Americans doing in other countries? ....
2. What was Lisa trying to buy? ....
3. How do people show "yes" in Micronesia? ....
4. Who was Jan talking to? ....
5. What does a head nod mean in Bulgaria? ....
6. Why did Tom misunderstand his class? ....

B What or who do these words refer to? Write the correct word(s).

1. it (par. 1, line 2)   ....
2. their (par. 1, line 4)   ....
3. her (par. 2, line 14, first word)   ....
4. that country (par. 3, line 6)   ....
5. the same thing (par. 4, line 10)   ....

C **GROUP WORK** Have you ever had a similar communication problem, or do you know someone who has? What happened?

Could you do me a favor? ■ 21

4 What a story!

1 SNAPSHOT

Popular Online News Categories   Search

Top Stories | Entertainment | Sports | Art | Travel | Opinion

World
Politics
Business
Technology
Science
Health
Odd News

New Species of Frog Discovered in Amazon

Source: http://news.yahoo.com

In your opinion, which sections contain the most interesting news? the least interesting news?
Choose five categories. Give an example of a possible type of story for each one.
Where do you get your news? What's happening in the news today?

2 PERSPECTIVES *Surprise endings*

A ▶ Listen to the news stories. In which news category from Exercise 1 do you think each story belongs?

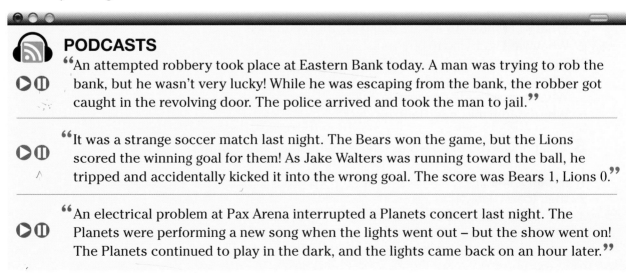

PODCASTS

"An attempted robbery took place at Eastern Bank today. A man was trying to rob the bank, but he wasn't very lucky! While he was escaping from the bank, the robber got caught in the revolving door. The police arrived and took the man to jail."

"It was a strange soccer match last night. The Bears won the game, but the Lions scored the winning goal for them! As Jake Walters was running toward the ball, he tripped and accidentally kicked it into the wrong goal. The score was Bears 1, Lions 0."

"An electrical problem at Pax Arena interrupted a Planets concert last night. The Planets were performing a new song when the lights went out – but the show went on! The Planets continued to play in the dark, and the lights came back on an hour later."

B **PAIR WORK** What happened in each story that was surprising?

3 GRAMMAR FOCUS

Past continuous vs. simple past ▶

Use the past continuous for an ongoing action in the past.
Use the simple past for an event that interrupts that action.

Past continuous	Simple past *catch*
While he **was escaping** from the bank,	the robber **got caught** in the revolving door.
As Jake **was running** toward the ball,	he **tripped** and **kicked** it into the wrong goal.
The Planets **were performing** a song	when the lights **went** out.

A Complete the news stories using the past continuous or simple past forms of the verbs. Then compare with a partner.

DAILY ROUNDUP

A Golden Find

While divers _were working_ (work) off the coast of Florida, they _discovered_ (discover) a shipwreck containing gold worth $2 million. The divers _were filming_ (film) a show about the coral reef when they _found_ (find) the gold.

Four-legged Customers

One windy day, a woman _was walking_ (walk) her pet poodle down the street. A hairstylist _saw_ (see) the dog through a window and _noticed_ (notice) its crazy hair! Later, while the stylist _was creating_ (create) a new line of hair care products for dogs and cats, he _came up with_ (come up with) a new slogan: "Even animals have bad hair days!"

Rescue… the Ambulance!

An ambulance driver _was having_ (have) breakfast in a coffee shop when a woman _hopped_ (hop) into his ambulance and _drove_ (drive) away. The driver _grabbed_ (grab) his cell phone and _alerted_ (alert) the police. The carjacker _was going_ (go) over 90 miles an hour when the highway patrol finally _caught up with_ (catch up with) her.

B **GROUP WORK** Take turns retelling the stories in part A. Add your own ideas and details to make the stories more interesting!

4 PRONUNCIATION *Intonation in complex sentences*

A Listen and practice. Notice how each clause in a complex sentence has its own intonation pattern.

While divers were working off the coast of Florida, they discovered a shipwreck.

As Jake was running toward the ball, he tripped and kicked it into the wrong goal.

B **PAIR WORK** Use your imagination to make complex sentences. Take turns starting and finishing the sentences. Pay attention to intonation.

A: While Sam was traveling in South America . . .
B: . . . he ran into an old friend in Lima.

5 LISTENING In the news

A ▶ Listen to three news stories. Number the pictures from 1 to 3.
(There is one extra picture.)

B ▶ Listen again. Take notes on each story.

Where did it happen?	When did it happen?	What happened?
1.	....	....
2.	....	....
3.	....	....

6 WRITING A news story

A Match each headline with the beginning of a news story.

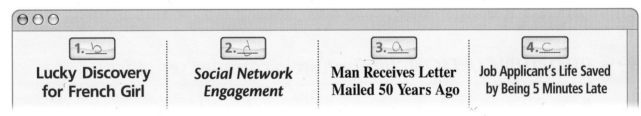

1. b
2. d
3. a
4. c

Lucky Discovery for French Girl
Social Network Engagement
Man Receives Letter Mailed 50 Years Ago
Job Applicant's Life Saved by Being 5 Minutes Late

a. Rick Jones got a surprise when he went to his mailbox last week.
b. Sophie Denis was playing in her yard when she found 30 Roman coins.
c. Lisa Miller is lucky. As she was hurrying to a job interview, she missed her bus.
d. Derek Adams didn't propose to his longtime girlfriend in the traditional way. He did it online.

B Complete one of the news stories from part A, or write a news story using your own idea. First, answer these questions. Then write your article.

Who was involved?   Where did it happen?
When did it happen?   What happened?

C **GROUP WORK** Take turns telling your stories. Other students ask questions. Who has the best story?

7 CONVERSATION *What happened?*

A ▶ Listen and practice.

Brian: Guess what! Someone stole my wallet last night!
Kathy: Oh, no! What happened?
Brian: Well, I was working out, and I had put my stuff in my locker, just like I always do. When I came back, someone had stolen my wallet. I guess I'd forgotten to lock the locker.
Kathy: That's terrible! Did you lose much money?
Brian: Only about $15. But I lost my credit card and my driver's license. What a pain!

B ▶ Listen to the rest of the conversation. What did Kathy have stolen once? Where was she?

8 GRAMMAR FOCUS

> ### Past perfect ▶
>
> **Use the past perfect for an event that occurred before another event in the past.**
>
> *I, you, we, they have / had*
> *she, he, it has / had*
>
> | Past event | Past perfect event |
> |---|---|
> | I **was working out,** | and I **had put** my stuff in my locker. |
> | When I **came back,** | someone **had stolen** my wallet. |
> | They **were able** to steal it | because I **had forgotten** to lock the locker. |

A Complete the sentences in column A with the simple past or past continuous forms of the verbs. Complete the sentences in column B with the simple past or past perfect forms of the verbs.

A

1. A thief _had broken into_ (break into) our house last night while my sister and I _were picking up_ (pick up) a pizza for dinner.
2. I _was shopping_ (shop) with some friends yesterday, and I _lost_ (lose) my keys.
3. I _was driving_ (drive) around with friends all day on Sunday, and I _ran out_ (run out) of gas on the freeway.
4. I _was trying_ (try) to visit my parents last night when I _got_ (get) stuck in the elevator in their apartment building.

B

a. Luckily, I _had given_ (give) a friend a copy of them, and she _came over_ (come over) and let me into my apartment.
b. It _reached_ (reach) the fifth floor when it _stopped_ (stop). After I _was_ (be) stuck for an hour, someone _started_ (start) it again.
c. I guess we _had left_ (leave) the door unlocked because that's how the thief _got_ (get) into the house.
d. Fortunately, I _had brought_ (bring) my cell phone with me, so I _called_ (call) my brother for help.

B PAIR WORK Match the sentences in parts A and B to make complete stories. Read them aloud.

1. _c_   2. _a_   3. _d_   4. _b_

9 WORD POWER Events

A Match the words in column A with the definitions in column B.

A

1. coincidence ....f....
2. dilemma ....b....
3. disaster ....d....
4. emergency ....g....
5. lucky break ....a....
6. misfortune ....h....
7. mystery ....c....
8. triumph ....e....

B

a. an unexpected event that brings good fortune
b. a situation that involves a difficult choice
c. something puzzling or unexplained
d. an event that causes suffering or destruction
e. a great success or achievement
f. unexpected events that seem to be connected
g. a sudden, dangerous event that requires quick action
h. an unlucky event, or bad luck

B PAIR WORK Choose one kind of event from part A. Write a situation for it.

> Two people were traveling separately in China when they met at a restaurant in Shanghai. They both lived in the same town their whole lives, but they had never met before. (coincidence)

C GROUP WORK Read your situation. Can others guess which kind of event it describes?

10 SPEAKING Tell me more.

GROUP WORK Have you ever had any of these experiences? Tell your group about it. Answer any questions.

I . . .
faced a dilemma
had an emergency
was unable to solve a mystery
had a lucky break
had a personal triumph

A: I faced a dilemma last week.
B: Really? What was it?
A: I got two job offers. I could take either a job with a large, successful company for a low salary or one with a smaller, less successful company for more pay.
C: So what did you decide to do?

11 INTERCHANGE 4 A double ending

Solve a mystery! Go to Interchange 4 on page 117.

The changing world of blogging

Scan the article. Who blogs? How is blogging changing?

Only a few years ago, blogging seemed new and exciting. Now, some people are saying it is yesterday's news and that the Internet revolution is moving on. The word "blog" comes from "web log," which means an online log or diary. Blogging is interactive, and bloggers hope that their readers will respond with interesting posts. In turn, they can respond to these posts. Some blogs continue like this for years whereas others simply vanish overnight. Blogs are usually started by one person for personal or professional reasons.

Anyone is free to blog: individuals, celebrities, companies, journalists. When blogging started, it was the first time ordinary people could write whatever they wanted and then e-publish it for the entire online world to see. Some people have become famous as bloggers, such as Julie Powell. Some celebrities have blogs, such as John Mayer and TV chef Jamie Oliver. Some companies, such as Microsoft and Boeing, use blogs to communicate with their employees. Journalists and broadcasters also write blogs. These are often on news websites, such as those for the *New York Times* and CNN.

However, things change fast with information technology. For many people, especially young people, social networking sites like Facebook have superseded blogging. In any case, there have always been far more blog readers than blog writers,

Julie Powell

perhaps because some people don't like writing. But developments in technology have changed blogging, too. With a videophone, camera, or camcorder plus a computer with video-editing software, bloggers can turn their blogs into video logs, or "vlogs." Some people think vlogging will replace blogging. Others disagree, saying that television didn't replace radio and that e-commerce hasn't stopped people from going shopping. What do *you* think?

A Read the article. Find the words in *italics* in the article.
Then check (✓) the meaning of each word.

1. *moving on*	☐ going backward	☑ doing something new
2. *vanish*	☐ continue to grow	☑ disappear
3. *entire*	☑ whole	☐ international
4. *broadcasters*	☑ TV or radio news reporters	☐ people who write news stories
5. *superseded*	☑ replaced	☐ became more exciting than
6. *e-commerce*	☐ electronic communication	☑ buying and selling online

B **PAIR WORK** Discuss these questions.

Why do some people think that blogging is no longer exciting?
What are some ways to maintain a blog successfully?
Do you think blogs are a good way to sell things? Why or why not?
Why have some people switched from blogging to social networking sites?

C **GROUP WORK** Do you read any blogs? Have you ever posted a message on one?
Why or why not?

Units 3–4 Progress check

SELF-ASSESSMENT

How well can you do these things? Check (✓) the boxes.

I can	Very well	OK	A little
Make and respond to requests (Ex. 1)	☐	☐	☐
Pass on messages (Ex. 2)	☐	☐	☐
Tell a story, making clear the sequence of events (Ex. 3, 5)	☐	☐	☐
Understand the sequence of events in a story (Ex. 4)	☐	☐	☐

1 ROLE PLAY *Planning a party*

Student A: You are planning a class party at your house. Think of three things you need help with. Then call a classmate and ask for help.

Student B: Student A is planning a party. Agree to help with some things, but not everything.

"Hi, Dave. I'm calling about the party. Would you mind . . . ?"

Change roles and try the role play again.

2 DISCUSSION *Mystery messages*

A GROUP WORK Take turns reading each request. Then discuss the questions and come up with possible answers.

> I'm sorry to bother you, but if Mr. Wall in Apartment 213 uses my space again, I'll have to complain to the manager.

> I'd really like to borrow it for the match on Friday. Please tell Tom to let me know soon if it's OK.

> Tell your officers that she's brown and has a red collar but no tag. She answers to the name "Lady." Call if you find her.

1. What is the situation?
2. Who is the request for? Who do you think received the request and passed it on?
3. Give an indirect request for each situation.

"Please tell Mr. Wall . . ."

B CLASS ACTIVITY Compare your answers. Which group has the most interesting answers for each message?

3 SPEAKING *What happened?*

A **PAIR WORK** Choose a type of event from the box. Then make up a title for a story about it. Write the title on a piece of paper.

> disaster   emergency   lucky break   mystery   triumph

B **PAIR WORK** Exchange titles with another pair. Discuss the questions *who, what, where, when, why,* and *how* about the other pair's title. Then make up a story.

C Share your story with the pair who wrote the title.

> **Dog Show Disaster**
> My brother recently entered his pet, Poofi, in a dog show. But Poofi is a cat! He was bringing Poofi into the show when . . .

4 LISTENING *What comes first?*

▶ Listen to each situation. Number the events from 1 to 3.

1. ☐ She hurt her ankle.   ☐ She was running.   ☐ She went to work.
2. ☐ John wrote to me.   ☐ I didn't get the letter.   ☐ I moved away.
3. ☐ I was very scared.   ☐ The plane landed.   ☐ I was relieved.
4. ☐ We went out.   ☐ My cousin stopped by.   ☐ I was watching a movie.

5 DISCUSSION *From A to B*

GROUP WORK Choose the beginning of a story from column A and an ending from column B. Discuss interesting or unusual events that could link A to B. Then make up a story.

A

Once, I . . .

received an unexpected phone call.
was asked to do an unusual favor.
accepted an interesting invitation.
owed someone a big apology.

B

Believe it or not, . . .

I opened the door, and a horse was standing there!
when I got there, everyone had left.
he didn't even remember what I had done.
it was the star of my favorite TV show!

A: Once, I received an unexpected phone call.
B: Let's see. . . . I was making coffee when the phone rang.
C: It was early in the morning, and I had just gotten up.
D: I had not completely woken up yet, but . . .

WHAT'S NEXT?

Look at your Self-assessment again. Do you need to review anything?

5 Crossing cultures

1 PERSPECTIVES *If I moved to a foreign country ...*

A ▶ Listen to the people talk about moving to a foreign country. Would you have any of the same concerns?

.... "One thing I'd really miss is my mom's cooking."

.... "I'd be worried about the local food. I might not like it."

.... "Getting used to different customs might be difficult at first."

.... "My room at home is the thing that I'd miss the most."

.... "Not knowing the prices of things is something I'd be concerned about."

.... "Moving to a country with a very different climate could be a challenge."

.... "I'd be worried about getting sick and not knowing how to find a good doctor."

.... "Something I'd be nervous about is communicating in a new language."

B Rate each concern from 1 (not worried at all) to 5 (really worried). What would be your biggest concern? Why?

2 WORD POWER *Culture shock*

A These words are used to describe how people sometimes feel when they live in a foreign country. Which are positive (**P**)? Which are negative (**N**)?

curious

anxious	embarrassed	insecure ....
comfortable	enthusiastic	nervous ....
confident	excited	uncertain ....
curious	fascinated	uncomfortable ....
depressed	homesick	worried ....

B GROUP WORK Tell your group about other situations in which you experienced the feelings in part A. What made you feel that way? How do you feel about the situations now?

A: I felt anxious yesterday. I had to give an important presentation at work.
B: How did the presentation go?
A: I was nervous and uncomfortable at first. I don't like speaking in public.
C: How did you feel after the presentation?
A: Actually, I felt pretty confident. I think it went really well!

3 GRAMMAR FOCUS

> ### Noun phrases containing relative clauses ▶
>
> **One thing (that) I'd really miss** is my mom's cooking.
> **Something (that) I'd be nervous about** is communicating in a new language.
> **Two people (who/that) I'd call every week** are my parents.
>
> My mom's cooking is **one thing (that) I'd really miss**.
> Communicatng in a new language is **something (that) I'd be nervous about**.
> My parents are **two people (who/that) I'd call every week**.

A Complete the sentences about living in a foreign country. Use the phrases below. Then compare with a partner.

my friends	trying new foods	making new friends	getting lost in a new city
my family	my favorite food	being away from home	not understanding people
getting sick	my room at home	speaking a new language	getting used to a different culture

1. One thing I'd definitely be excited about is . . .
2. . . . is something I'd really miss.
3. Two things I'd be homesick for are . . .
4. . . . are two things I'd be anxious about.
5. Something I'd get depressed about is . . .
6. . . . is one thing that I might be embarrassed about.
7. The thing I'd feel most uncomfortable about would be . . .
8. . . . are the people who I'd miss the most.
9. One thing I'd be insecure about is . . .
10. . . . are two things I'd be very enthusiastic about.

B Now complete three sentences in part A with your own information.

C **GROUP WORK** Rewrite your sentences from part B in another way. Then compare. Do others feel the same way?

1. One thing I'd definitely be excited about is taking pictures as I go sightseeing.

4 PRONUNCIATION *Word stress in sentences*

A ▶ Listen and practice. Notice that the important words in a sentence have more stress.

●   ●   ●
Argentina is a country that I'd like to live in.

●   ●   ●   ●
Speaking a new language is something I'd be anxious about.

●   ●   ●   ●
Trying new foods is something I'd be curious about.

B **PAIR WORK** Mark the stress in the sentences you wrote in Exercise 3, part A. Then practice the sentences. Pay attention to word stress.

GROUP WORK Read the questions. Think of two more questions to add to the list. Then take turns asking and answering the questions in groups.

What country would you like to live in? Why?
What country wouldn't you like to live in? Why?
Who is the person you would most like to go abroad with?
What is something you would never travel without?
Who is the person you would email first after arriving somewhere new?
What would be your two greatest concerns about living abroad?
What is the thing you would enjoy the most about living abroad?

A: What country would you like to live in?
B: The country I'd most like to live in is Italy.
C: Why is that?
B: Well, I've always wanted to study art.

6 **SNAPSHOT**

DIFFERENT CUSTOMS

Canada
If you are invited for a meal, you should arrive on time – not early or late.

Indonesia
Never point to anything with your foot.

Thailand
Never touch anyone – especially a child – on the head.

Brazil
Open any gift in front of the person who gave it to you.

South Korea
Always use both hands to pass something to an older person.

Egypt
Don't eat anything with your left hand.

France
When eating out, keep both hands on or above the table.

Nigeria
When you meet people, don't call them by their first names until they say you can.

Sources: *Kiss, Bow, or Shake Hands*; www.kwintessential.co.uk

Does your culture follow any of these customs?
Do any of these customs seem unusual to you? Explain.
What other interesting customs do you know?

7 CONVERSATION *What's the custom?*

A ▶ Listen and practice.

Marta: I just got invited to my teacher's house for dinner.
Karen: Oh, how nice!
Marta: Yes, but what do you do here when you're invited to someone's house?
Karen: Well, here in the U.S., it's the custom to bring a small gift.
Marta: Like what?
Karen: Oh, maybe some flowers or chocolates.
Marta: And is it all right to bring a friend along?
Karen: Well, if you want to bring someone, you're expected to call first and ask if it's OK.

B ▶ Listen to the rest of the conversation. If you are invited to someone's house in Germany, when are you expected to arrive? What can you bring as a gift?

8 GRAMMAR FOCUS

Expectations ▶

When you visit someone,	it**'s the custom to** bring a small gift. you **aren't supposed to** arrive early.
If you want to bring someone,	you**'re expected to** call first and ask. you**'re supposed to** check with the host. it**'s not acceptable to** arrive without calling first.

A Match information in columns A and B to make sentences about customs in the United States and Canada. Then compare with a partner.

A

1. If you plan to visit someone at home, ...
2. If you've been to a friend's home for dinner, ...
3. When you have been invited to a wedding, ...
4. When you go out on a date, ...
5. If the service in a restaurant is acceptable, ...
6. When you meet someone for the first time, ...

B

a. you're supposed to call first.
b. you're expected to leave a tip.
c. you aren't supposed to kiss him or her.
d. you're expected to respond in writing.
e. it's the custom to thank him or her.
f. it's acceptable to share the expenses.

B **GROUP WORK** How are the customs in part A different in your country?

C Complete these sentences with information about your country or a country you know well. Then compare with a partner.

1. In . . . , if people invite you to their home, . . .
2. When you go out with friends for dinner, . . .
3. If a friend gets engaged to be married, . . .
4. When a relative has a birthday, . . .
5. If a friend is in the hospital, . . .
6. When someone is going to have a baby, . . .

Crossing cultures ▪ 33

9 LISTENING Unique customs

▶ Listen to people describe customs they observed abroad. Complete the chart.

	Where was the person?	What was the custom?	How did the person react?
1. Alice	....	....	....
2. John	....	....	....
3. Susan	....	....	....

10 SPEAKING Things to remember

A **PAIR WORK** What should a visitor to your country know about local customs? Make a list. Include these points.

greeting someone   dressing appropriately
eating in public   visiting someone's home
taking photographs   traveling by bus or train
shopping   tipping

B **GROUP WORK** Compare your lists with another pair. Then share experiences in which you (or someone you know) *didn't* follow the appropriate cultural behavior. What happened?

A: On my last vacation, I tried to bargain for something in a store.
B: What happened?
A: I was told that the prices were fixed. It was a little embarrassing because . . .

11 WRITING A tourist pamphlet

A **GROUP WORK** Choose five points from the list you made in Exercise 10. Use them to write and design a tourist pamphlet for your country.

Tips for Travelers
When you visit Indonesia, there are some important things you should know. For example, if you are visiting a mosque or temple, it's not acceptable to take photographs. Also, you are supposed to . . .

B **CLASS ACTIVITY** Present your pamphlets. Would a visitor to your country have all the information he or she needed?

12 INTERCHANGE 5 Culture check

Compare customs in different countries. Go to Interchange 5 on page 118.

BLOG

CULTURE SHOCK

Scan the blog. What kinds of culture shock did the writer experience?

Kit-ken Lim, a student from Taipei, Taiwan, is studying in Chicago. The following entries are taken from her blog during her first three months in the United States.

August 31

People often refer to Taipei as "The Sleepless City," but I didn't understand why until I got to Chicago. I was window-shopping with another student this evening. Suddenly, the store owners started pulling down their gates and locking their doors. Soon the whole street was closed. And it wasn't even dark yet! I'd never seen this in Taiwan. Back home, the busiest streets "stay awake" all night. You can go out to restaurants, stores, and movies even long after midnight. **MORE**

September 5

After the first week of class, I've found some differences between Taiwanese students and American students. Whenever a teacher asks a question, my classmates immediately shout out their answers. And some of them interrupt the teacher. In Taiwan, we're usually quiet in class so that the teacher can finish on time. We usually ask the teacher questions afterward. American students seem to leave the room as soon as the class ends. **MORE**

October 6

I met an interesting girl at an Internet café today. I was writing an email to my mother, and she asked me what language I was using. We ended up talking for about an hour! People in Chicago seem very comfortable with each other. It's very natural for two people to start talking in a café. This is something that doesn't happen in Taipei. At home, I'd never just start chatting with a stranger. I like that it's easy to meet new people here. **MORE**

A Read the blog. Then add the correct title to each blog entry.

Café etiquette   Less than 24/7   Just say it!

B Complete the chart.

	Chicago	Taipei
1. When does the city shut down?		
2. How do students behave in class?		
3. How do students behave after class?		
4. How do people act toward strangers?		

C **PAIR WORK** How do things in your city compare with Taipei? with Chicago?

6 What's wrong with it?

Some Common Complaints

Wireless service
There is no signal, so you can't get online.

Hotels
The bathroom sink is leaking.

Cleaners
The dry cleaner shrinks your favorite sweater.

Taxis
The driver tries to charge you too much.

Doctors
You have to wait a long time for your appointment.

Restaurants
Your food is undercooked.

Source: Based on information from *The Great American Gripe Book*

Have you ever had any of these complaints? Which ones?
What would you do in each of these situations?
What other complaints have you had?

2 PERSPECTIVES

A ▶ Listen to people describe complaints on a call-in radio show.
Check (✓) what you think each person should do.

Ask Priscilla
the
Problem
Solver!

❶ "I ordered a jacket online, but when it arrived, I found the lining was torn."
☐ ask for a refund ☐ send it back and get a new one

❷ "I bought a new table from a store, but when they delivered it, I noticed it was damaged on the top."
☐ ask for a discount ☐ ask the store to replace it

❸ "A friend sent me a vase for my birthday, but when it arrived, it was chipped."
☐ tell her about it ☐ say nothing and repair it yourself

❹ "I lent a friend my sunglasses, and now there are scratches on the lenses."
☐ say nothing ☐ ask him to replace them

❺ "I took some pants to the cleaners, and when they came back, they had a stain on them."
☐ wash them by hand ☐ ask the cleaners to wash them again for free

B Have you ever had similar complaints? What happened? What did you do?

Describing problems 1 ▶

With past participles as adjectives

The jacket lining is **torn**.
The tabletop is **damaged**.
That vase is **chipped**.
My pants are **stained**.
Her sunglasses are a little **scratched**.
The sink **is leaking**.*

With nouns

It has **a tear** in it./There's **a hole** in it.
There is **some damage** on the top.
There is **a chip** in it.
They have **a stain** on them.
There are **a few scratches** on them.
It has **a leak**.

Exception: is leaking *is a present continuous form.*

A Read the comments from customers in a restaurant. Write sentences in two different ways using forms of the word in parentheses. Then compare with a partner.

1. This tablecloth isn't very clean. It . . . (stain)
2. Could we have another water pitcher? This one . . . (leak)
3. The table looks pretty dirty. The wood . . . , too. (scratch)
4. The waiter needs a new shirt. The one he's wearing . . . (tear)
5. Could you bring me another cup of coffee? This cup . . . (chip)
6. The walls really need paint. And the ceiling . . . (damage)

> 1. It's stained.
>   It has a stain on it.

B **PAIR WORK** Describe two problems with each thing below. Use forms of the words in the box. You may use the same word more than once.

break	crack	damage	dent	leak	scratch	stain	tear

A: The car is dented.
B: Yes. And the paint is scratched.

C **GROUP WORK** Look around your classroom. How many problems can you describe?

"The floor is scratched, and the window is cracked. The desks are . . ."

4 LISTENING Fair exchange?

A ▶ Listen to three customers return an item they purchased. What's the problem? Take notes. Then complete the chart.

Item	Problem	Will the store exchange it?	
		Yes	**No**
1.	....	☐	☐
2.	....	☐	☐
3.	....	☐	☐

B Were the solutions fair? Why or why not?

5 ROLE PLAY What's the problem?

Student A: You are returning an item to a store. Decide what the item is and explain why you are returning it.

Student B: You are a salesperson. A customer is returning an item to the store. Ask these questions:

What exactly is the problem?
Can you show it to me?
Was it like this when you bought it?

When did you buy it?
Do you have the receipt?
Would you like a refund or a store credit?

Change roles and try the role play again.

6 CONVERSATION It keeps burning!

A ▶ Listen and practice.

Ms. Lock: Hello?
Mr. Burr: Hello, Ms. Lock. This is Jack Burr.
Ms. Lock: Uh, Mr. Burr . . .
Mr. Burr: In Apartment 305.
Ms. Lock: Oh, yes. What can I do for you? Does your refrigerator need fixing again?
Mr. Burr: No, it's the oven this time.
Ms. Lock: Oh, so what's wrong with it?
Mr. Burr: Well, I think the temperature control needs to be adjusted. The oven keeps burning everything I try to cook.
Ms. Lock: Really? OK, I'll have someone look at it right away.
Mr. Burr: Thanks a lot, Ms. Lock.
Ms. Lock: Uh, by the way, Mr. Burr, are you sure it's the oven and not your cooking?

B ▶ Listen to another tenant calling Ms. Lock. What's the tenant's problem?

7 GRAMMAR FOCUS

Describing problems 2 ▶

Need + *gerund*	Need + *passive infinitive*	Keep + *gerund*
The oven **needs adjusting**.	It **needs to be adjusted**.	Everything **keeps burning**.
The alarm **needs fixing**.	It **needs to be fixed**.	The alarm **keeps going off**.

A What needs to be done in this apartment? Write sentences about these items using *need* with gerunds or passive infinitives.

1. the walls (paint)
2. the rug (clean)
3. the windows (wash)
4. the clothes (pick up)
5. the lamp shade (replace)
6. the wastebasket (empty)
7. the ceiling fan (adjust)
8. the plant (water)

> 1. The walls need painting.
> OR
> 1. The walls need to be painted.

B PAIR WORK Think of five improvements you would like to make in your home. Which improvements will you most likely make? Which won't you make?

"First, the smoke alarm in the kitchen needs replacing. It keeps going off. . . ."

8 WORD POWER Electronics

A Circle the correct gerund to complete the sentences. Then compare with a partner.

1. My TV screen goes on and off all the time. It keeps **flickering / sticking**.
2. That old DVD player often jumps to another scene. It keeps **crashing / skipping**.
3. The battery in my new camera doesn't last long. It keeps **freezing / dying**.
4. The buttons on the remote control don't work well. They keep **skipping / sticking**.
5. Something is very wrong with my computer! It keeps **jamming / crashing**.
6. This printer isn't making all the copies I want. It keeps **jamming / flickering**.
7. My computer screen needs to be replaced. It keeps **dropping / freezing**.
8. I can't make long calls on my new phone. They keep **dying / dropping**.

B GROUP WORK Describe a problem with an electronic item you own. Don't identify it! Others will try to guess the item.

"Something I own keeps jamming. It happens when I'm driving. . . ."

9 PRONUNCIATION *Contrastive stress*

A ▶ Listen and practice. Notice how a change in stress changes the meaning of each question and elicits a different response.

Is the bedroom window cracked?   (No, the kitchen window is cracked.)

Is the bedroom window cracked?   (No, the bedroom door is cracked.)

Is the bedroom window cracked?   (No, it's broken.)

B ▶ Listen to the questions. Check (✓) the correct response.

1. a. Are my jeans torn?
   - ☐ No, they're stained.
   - ☐ No, your shirt is torn.

   b. Are my jeans torn?
   - ☐ No, they're stained.
   - ☐ No, your shirt is torn.

2. a. Is the computer screen flickering?
   - ☐ No, it's freezing.
   - ☐ No, the TV screen is flickering.

   b. Is the computer screen flickering?
   - ☐ No, it's freezing.
   - ☐ No, the TV screen is flickering.

10 LISTENING *Repair jobs*

▶ Listen to three people talk about their jobs. Complete the chart.

	What does this person repair?	What is the typical problem?
1. Joe		
2. Louise		
3. Sam		

11 WRITING *A critical online review*

A Imagine that you ordered a product online, but when you received it, you were unhappy with it. Write a critical online review. Explain all of the problems with the product and why you think others shouldn't buy it.

B **GROUP WORK** Read your classmates' reviews. What would you do if you read this critical online review and worked for the company that sold the product?

DON'T BUY
from **Games and Things!**

Last month I ordered a new joystick for my video game system online. First, it took way too long for the company to send it to me. Then, after using it for a few weeks, I discovered it was damaged. It keeps sticking and . . . READ MORE

12 INTERCHANGE 6 *Fixer-upper*

Do you have an eye for detail? Student A, go to Interchange 6A on page 119; Student B, go to Interchange 6B on page 120.

THE VALUE OF UPCYCLING

Scan the article. What is "upcycling"? Why are some people trying to promote it?

Recycling is a well-known idea that refers to reusing waste materials in any way possible. But what about "upcycling"? It's a new word, even though it's something that has been going on since human civilization began. It means reusing waste materials so that they have greater value. Throughout history, people have always done creative things with "trash." For example, they've used straw and dead leaves to make roofs, skin from dead animals to make leather goods, and wood from fallen trees to make boats. So why is there a new word for it now?

One answer to this question is that we reuse fewer and fewer things, and so we have become a "throwaway" society. This has raised huge questions about waste: Where can we dump it all? Will it pollute the environment? Could it endanger our health? The evidence is everywhere – even in the Pacific Ocean, where billions of bits of broken plastic float near the surface. Fish eat them, and then we eat the fish.

So upcyclers have adopted this new word to focus people's attention on how waste cannot simply be reused, but be reused profitably. In fact, upcyclers don't like the idea of waste and prefer to call it an "asset," something of value. Nowadays, there are lots of organizations that market products with upcycled material. Some artists and designers have upcycled things like denim from old jeans to make rugs, and wood from old houses to make furniture. Others have even used old magazines to make stools, and candy wrappers to make handbags! Sometimes they'll add a stylish element to their products, such as a beautiful mosaic made with chipped or broken dishes. With an endless supply of "assets," it seems that upcycling has a great future.

A Read the article. Then for each statement, check (✓) True, False, or Not given.

	True	False	Not given
1. Upcycling is a new kind of recycling.	☐	☐	☐
2. People have always used wood to build houses.	☐	☐	☐
3. A "throwaway" society is careful to reuse things.	☐	☐	☐
4. The Atlantic Ocean is full of pieces of broken plastic.	☐	☐	☐
5. Some people make money by upcycling.	☐	☐	☐
6. Artists are not interested in upcycling.	☐	☐	☐

B Look at the photos. What do you think each product is made of?

car parts	chopsticks	pants	safety pins	wooden boards

1. .... 2. .... 3. .... 4. .... 5. ....

C GROUP WORK Do you own anything that is made from upcycled material?
If so, what is it? What do you think of the idea of upcycling? Explain your opinion.

Units 5–6 Progress check

SELF-ASSESSMENT

How well can you do these things? Check (✓) the boxes.

I can	Very well	OK	A little
Describe a range of emotions (Ex. 1)	☐	☐	☐
Give opinions about behavior (Ex. 2)	☐	☐	☐
Understand problems and complaints (Ex. 3)	☐	☐	☐
Describe problems with physical objects (e.g., a car) (Ex. 4)	☐	☐	☐
Describe problematic situations (e.g., in a school) (Ex. 5)	☐	☐	☐

 SPEAKING *How would you feel?*

PAIR WORK Choose a situation. Then ask your partner questions about it using the words in the box. Take turns.

getting married   starting a new job
meeting your hero   going to a new school

anxious	excited
curious	insecure
embarrassed	nervous
enthusiastic	worried

A: If you were getting married tomorrow, what would you be anxious about?
B: One thing I'd be anxious about is the vows. I'd be worried about saying the wrong thing!

2 SURVEY *What's acceptable?*

A What do you think of these behaviors? Complete the survey.

Is it acceptable to . . . ?	Yes	No	It depends
kiss in public	☐	☐	☐
ask how old someone is	☐	☐	☐
call your parents by their first names	☐	☐	☐
use a cell phone in a restaurant	☐	☐	☐
put your feet on the furniture	☐	☐	☐

B **GROUP WORK** Compare your opinions. When are these behaviors acceptable? When are they unacceptable? What behaviors are never acceptable?

A: It's not acceptable to kiss in public.
B: Oh, I think it depends. In my country, if you're greeting someone, it's the custom to kiss on the cheek.

3 LISTENING Complaints

A ▶ Listen to three tenants complain to their building manager. Complete the chart.

Tenants' complaints	How the problems are solved
1.	....
2.	....
3.	....

B GROUP WORK Do you agree with the solutions? How would you solve the problems?

4 ROLE PLAY Haggling

Student A: Imagine you are buying this car from Student B, but it's too expensive. Describe the problems you see to get a better price.

Student B: You are trying to sell this car, but it has some problems. Make excuses for the problems to get the most money.

A: I want to buy this car, but the body has a few scratches. I'll give you $ . . . for it.
B: That's no big deal. You can't really see them, anyway. How about $ . . . ?
A: Well, what about the seat? It's . . .
B: You can fix that easily. . . .

Change roles and try the role play again.

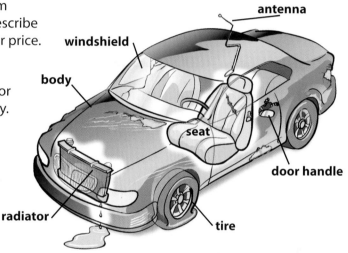

5 DISCUSSION School council meeting

A GROUP WORK Imagine you are on the school council. You are discussing improvements to your school. Decide on the five biggest issues.

A: The cafeteria food needs to be improved.
B: Yes, but it's more important to fix the computer in the lounge. It keeps crashing.

B CLASS ACTIVITY Share your list with the class. What are the three most needed improvements? Can you think of how to accomplish them?

WHAT'S NEXT?

Look at your Self-assessment again. Do you need to review anything?

7 The world we live in

Waste Not, Want Not

Some alarming facts

Americans . . . .

- make **750,000** photocopies every minute
- throw away **2.5 million** plastic bottles every hour
- get rid of **30,000** cars every day
- dispose of **49 million** baby diapers every day

- receive **4 million** tons of junk mail every year
- use **65 billion** aluminum cans every year
- throw out **270 million** tires every year

Source: www.cleanair.org

Which of the things above seem the most wasteful?
What do you throw away? What do you tend to recycle?
What are two other environmental problems that concern you?

2 PERSPECTIVES *Clean up our city!*

A ◉ Listen to an announcement from an election campaign.
What kinds of problems does Roberta Chang want to fix?

VOTE FOR ROBERTA CHANG CITY COUNCIL

Roberta Chang will clean up Cradville!
Have you noticed these problems in our city?

★ The air is being polluted by fumes from cars and trucks.

★ Potholes aren't being repaired due to a lack of funding.

★ The homeless have been displaced from city shelters because of overcrowding.

★ Many parks have been lost through overbuilding.

★ Our city streets are being damaged as a result of heavy traffic.

★ Our fresh water supply is being depleted through overuse by people who don't conserve.

☆ *A vote for Roberta Chang is a vote for solutions!* ☆

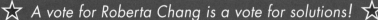

B Which of these problems affect your city? Can you give specific examples?

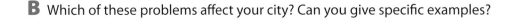

Passive with prepositions ⊙

Present continuous passive

The air is **being polluted**	**by** fumes from cars and trucks.
City streets **are being damaged**	**as a result of** heavy traffic.
Potholes **aren't being repaired**	**due to** a lack of funding.

Present perfect passive

Many parks **have been lost**	**through** overbuilding.
The homeless **have been displaced**	**because of** overcrowding in city shelters.

A **PAIR WORK** Match the photos of environmental problems with the sentences below.

1. Air pollution is threatening the health of people in urban areas. (by)
2. Livestock farms have contaminated soil and underground water. (because of)
3. Acid rain has eroded statues and buildings. (as a result of)
4. Oil spills are harming birds, fish, and other marine life. (through)
5. The growth of suburbs has eaten up huge amounts of farmland. (due to)
6. The destruction of rain forests is accelerating the extinction of plants and wildlife. (by)

B Rewrite the sentences in part A using the passive and the prepositions given. Then compare with a partner.

> 1. The health of people in urban areas is being threatened by air pollution.

C **PAIR WORK** Cover the sentences in part A above. Take turns describing the environmental problems in the pictures in your own words.

4 PRONUNCIATION *Reduction of auxiliary verbs*

A ▶ Listen and practice. Notice how the auxiliary verb forms **is**, **are**, **has**, and **have** are reduced in conversation.

Fresh water *is* being wasted.
Newspapers *are* being thrown away.

Too much trash *has* been created.
Parks *have* been lost.

B **PAIR WORK** Practice the sentences you wrote in Exercise 3, part B. Pay attention to the reduction of **is**, **are**, **has**, and **have**.

5 LISTENING *Environmental solutions*

A ▶ Listen to three people describe some serious environmental problems. Check (✓) the problem each person talks about.

Problem			What can be done about it?
1. Jenny	☐ landfills	☐ poor farmland	....
2. Adam	☐ electricity	☐ e-waste	....
3. Katy	☐ air pollution	☐ water pollution	....

B ▶ Listen again. What can be done to solve each problem? Complete the chart.

6 WORD POWER *World problems*

A **PAIR WORK** How concerned is your partner about these problems? Check (✓) his or her answers.

Problems	Very concerned	Fairly concerned	Not concerned
cancer	☐	☐	☐
drug trafficking	☐	☐	☐
famine	☐	☐	☐
global warming	☐	☐	☐
government corruption	☐	☐	☐
inflation	☐	☐	☐
overpopulation	☐	☐	☐
political unrest	☐	☐	☐
poverty	☐	☐	☐

B **GROUP WORK** Share your partner's answers with another pair. Which problems concern your group the most? What will happen if the problem isn't solved?

A: Many lives have been lost to due to cancer.
B: We need to find ways to raise money for more research.
C: I agree. If we don't, the disease will continue to spread.

7 CONVERSATION *What can we do?*

A ▶ Listen and practice.

Carla: Look at all those dead fish! What do you think happened?

Andy: Well, there's a factory outside town that's pumping chemicals into the river.

Carla: How can they do that? Isn't that against the law?

Andy: Yes, it is. But a lot of companies ignore those laws.

Carla: That's terrible! What can we do about it?

Andy: Well, one way to change things is to talk to the company's management.

Carla: What if that doesn't work?

Andy: Well, then another way to stop them is to get a TV station to run a story on it.

Carla: Yes! Companies hate bad publicity. By the way, what's the name of this company?

Andy: It's called Avox Industries.

Carla: Really? My uncle is one of their top executives.

B CLASS ACTIVITY What else could Andy and Carla do?

C ▶ Listen to the rest of the conversation. What do Andy and Carla decide to do?

8 GRAMMAR FOCUS

Infinitive clauses and phrases ▶

One way **to change** things is	**to talk** to the company's management.
Another way **to stop** them is	**to get** a TV station to run a story.
The best ways **to fight** cancer are	**to do** more research and educate people.

A Find one or more solutions for each problem. Then compare with a partner.

Problems

1. One way to reduce famine is ....
2. The best way to fight cancer is ....
3. One way to stop political unrest is ....
4. One way to improve air quality is ....
5. The best way to reduce poverty is ....
6. One way to help the homeless is ....

Solutions

a. to build more public housing.
b. to train people in modern farming methods.
c. to start free vocational training programs.
d. to educate people on healthy lifestyle choices.
e. to have more police on the streets.
f. to provide ways for people to voice their concerns.
g. to develop cleaner public transportation.
h. to create more jobs for the unemployed.

B GROUP WORK Can you think of two more solutions for each problem in part A? Agree on the best solution for each.

9 DISCUSSION Problems and solutions

A **PAIR WORK** Describe the problems shown in the photos.
Then make suggestions about how to solve these problems.

What can be done ...?

1. to stop drug trafficking
2. to improve children's health
3. to keep our parks clean
4. to reduce unemployment

A: Our economy is being ruined by drug trafficking.
B: Well, one way to stop it is . . .

B **CLASS ACTIVITY** Share your solutions. Which ones are the most innovative?
Which ones are most likely to solve the problems?

10 INTERCHANGE 7 *Make your voices heard!*

Brainstorm solutions to some local problems. Go to Interchange 7 on page 121.

11 WRITING *A message on a community website*

A Choose a problem from the unit or use one of your own ideas. Write a message
to post on a local community website.

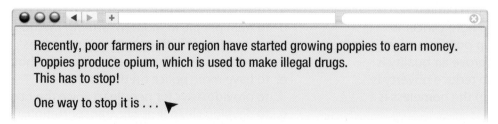

Recently, poor farmers in our region have started growing poppies to earn money.
Poppies produce opium, which is used to make illegal drugs.
This has to stop!

One way to stop it is . . . ▶

B **PAIR WORK** Exchange messages with a partner. Imagine you live in the same community.
Write a response suggesting another solution.

Saving a Coral Reef
An Eco Tipping Point

Scan the first two paragraphs. What was the problem for the people of Apo Island?

Nowadays, there seems to be so much bad news about the environment. Scientists have predicted all kinds of alarming ecological "tipping points." These are times when, for some reason, big changes happen suddenly, such as when farmland turns to desert due to climate change. But do tipping points inevitably go in the wrong direction?

Apo Island is nine kilometers off the coast of Negros in the Philippines, an area rich in coral reefs. Until the 1950s, local fishermen used traditional fishing methods and there were always lots of fish in the island's reef. Then the fishermen adopted new techniques. They used explosives to scare the fish out of their hiding places, cyanide to poison the fish, and fine nets to catch even very small fish. As a result, they caught more fish. So they increased their use of these techniques. Then there was a tipping point – almost no fish in the reef! So the fishermen had to go further out to sea to find enough fish.

In the 1980s, Dr. Angel Alcala, a marine scientist, visited Apo Island to help the fishermen solve the problem. One way to reverse the tipping point, he explained, was to create a no-fishing zone. The fishermen decided that almost 10 percent of the island's reef should become a sanctuary. After three years, the sanctuary was full of fish and the fishermen were able to catch lots of fish near its edge.

The fishermen were so impressed by this positive eco tipping point that they decided to stop all destructive fishing methods around the entire island. This ecological lesson is now part of the curriculum in the local school, and income from tourism is used to fund scholarships for local students to study marine ecosystem management. Moreover, Apo Island has become a model fishing community – 700 villages in the Philippines now have marine sanctuaries.

The Philippines
Manila
Apo Island

A Read the article. Then complete the chart with information from the article.

APO ISLAND'S NEGATIVE ECO TIPPING POINT
- Local fishermen adopted destructive fishing methods in the reef.
- _____
- They increased their use of destructive fishing methods.
- _____
- The fishermen had to go far out to sea to find enough fish.

APO ISLAND'S POSITIVE ECO TIPPING POINT
- The fishermen created a fish sanctuary in the reef.
- _____
- The fishermen could find enough fish in the reef.
- _____
- Marine ecosystem management was included in education.

B What can other communities with ecological problems learn from Apo Island?

Lifelong learning

1 SNAPSHOT

THE TEN MOST POPULAR COLLEGE MAJORS

1. **Business:** Learn about commerce, finance, marketing, and accounting.
2. **Social Sciences and History:** Study economics, geography, and sociology.
3. **Education:** Study how people learn and how best to teach them.
4. **Psychology:** Learn about human mental processes and behavior.
5. **Nursing:** Acquire the skills needed to take care of sick people.
6. **Communications:** Learn about journalism, new media, and human interaction.
7. **Biology:** Learn the fundamentals of life science.
8. **Engineering:** Study the application of math and science to practical ends.
9. **English:** Analyze works of literature written in the English language.
10. **Computer Science:** Study the theoretical foundations of computation and its applications.

Source: www.campusgrotto.com

*Which of these majors would be good for people who like technology?
like to work with others? like to be outside? like to solve problems?
Which ones sound the most interesting to you? Why?*

2 PERSPECTIVES

A ▶ Listen to the survey. Who is the survey targeting? What does the survey want to know?

Pick a subject!
We are expanding the school curriculum next year. What kinds of classes should we add? Please take a moment to answer a few questions.

1 Would you rather take a business class or a communications class?

- ○ I'd rather take a business class. (Go to question 2a.)
- ○ I'd rather take a communications class. (Go to question 2b.)
- ○ I'd rather take another type of course. (Go to question 3.)

2a Would you prefer to study commerce or marketing?

- ○ I'd prefer to study commerce.
- ○ I'd prefer to study marketing.
- ○ I'd prefer not to study either. I'd prefer another business course: [＿＿＿]

2b Would you rather study journalism or new media?

- ○ I'd rather study journalism.
- ○ I'd rather study new media.
- ○ I'd rather not study either. I'd prefer another communications course: [＿＿＿]

3 What other types of courses would you add to the curriculum? [＿＿＿]

B Take the survey. Be sure to fill in the blanks if necessary.

3 PRONUNCIATION Intonation in questions of choice

 Listen and practice. Notice the intonation in questions of choice.

Would you prefer to study nursing or education?   Would you rather be a psychologist or an engineer?

4 GRAMMAR FOCUS

Would rather *and* would prefer ▶

Would rather *takes the base form of the verb.* **Would prefer** *usually takes an infinitive. Both are followed by* not *in the negative.*

Would you **rather take** a business or communications class?
   I**'d rather take** a communications class.
   I**'d rather not take** either.
   I**'d rather take** another course **than study** business or communications.

Would you **prefer to study** business or communications?
   I**'d prefer to study** business.   I**'d prefer not to study** either.

Let's join a club.
   I**'d rather not join** a club.
   I**'d rather not**.
   I**'d prefer not to join** a club.
   I**'d prefer not to**.

A Complete the conversations with *would* and the appropriate form of the verbs in parentheses. Then practice with a partner.

1. A: .... you prefer .... (sign up) for a course in biology or geography?
   B: I'm not really interested in geography, so I'd prefer .... (take) a biology course.

2. A: .... you rather .... (learn) English in England or Canada?
   B: To tell you the truth, I'd prefer .... (not study) in either place. I'd rather .... (go) to Australia because it's warmer there.

3. A: If you needed to learn a new skill, ... you prefer .... (attend) a class or .... (have) a private tutor?
   B: I'd rather .... (take) a class than .... (hire) a tutor.

4. A: .... you rather .... (have) a job in an office or .... (work) outdoors?
   B: I'd definitely rather .... (have) a job where I'm outdoors.

B **PAIR WORK** Take turns asking the questions in part A. Pay attention to intonation. Give your own information when responding.

Lifelong learning ■ 51

5 LISTENING *Just for fun*

A ▶ Listen to three people talk about the part-time courses they took recently. What course did each person take?

	What course each person took	What each person learned
1. Linda	....	....
2. Rich	....	....
3. Gwen	....	....

B ▶ Listen again. What additional information did each person learn?

6 ROLE PLAY *Choose a major.*

Student A: Choose a major from the Snapshot on page 50 or use your own idea. Explain to Student B, your guidance counselor, why the major is the right choice for your future career.

Student B: You are Student A's guidance counselor. Convince Student A that he or she has chosen the wrong major. Give reasons why the major isn't right for him or her.

Change roles and try the role play again.

7 INTERCHANGE 8 *Learning curves*

What would your classmates like to learn? Take a survey. Go to Interchange 8 on page 122.

8 CONVERSATION *Maybe I should try that!*

A ▶ Listen and practice.

Won-gyu: So how's your French class going?

Kelly: Not bad, but I'm finding the pronunciation difficult.

Won-gyu: Well, I imagine it takes a while to get it right. You know, you could improve your accent by listening to language CDs.

Kelly: That's a good idea. But how do you learn new vocabulary? I always seem to forget new words.

Won-gyu: I learn new English words best by writing them on pieces of paper and sticking them on things in my room. I look at them every night before I go to sleep.

Kelly: Hmm. Maybe I should try something like that!

B ▶ Listen to two other people explain how they learn new words in a foreign language. What techniques do they use?

C CLASS ACTIVITY How do you learn new words in a foreign language?

9 GRAMMAR FOCUS

By + gerund to describe how to do things ▶

You could improve your accent **by listening** to language CDs.
I learn new words best **by writing** them on pieces of paper and **sticking** them on things.
The best way to learn slang is not **by watching** the news but **by watching** movies.

A How can you improve your English? Complete the sentences with *by* and the gerund forms of the verbs. Then compare with a partner.

1. You can improve your accent .... (mimic) native speakers.
2. A good way to learn idioms is .... (watch) videos online.
3. Students can become better writers .... (get) a private tutor.
4. A good way to learn new vocabulary is .... (access) a "learner's dictionary."
5. People can become faster readers .... (skim) magazines in English.
6. One way of practicing conversation is .... (role-play) with a partner in class.
7. You can learn to use grammar correctly .... (utilize) self-study materials.
8. The best way to develop self-confidence in speaking is .... (converse) with native speakers.

B **GROUP WORK** Complete the sentences in part A with your own ideas. What's the best suggestion for each item?

A: In my opinion, a good way to improve your accent is by watching sitcoms.
B: I think the best way is not by watching TV but by talking to native speakers.

10 DISCUSSION *Ways of learning*

A ▶ Listen to Todd and Lucy describe how they developed two skills. How did they learn? Complete the chart.

	Todd	Lucy
1. learn to play a musical instrument	....	....
2. become a good conversationalist	....	....

B **GROUP WORK** How would *you* learn to do the things in the chart?

C **GROUP WORK** Talk about different ways to learn to do each of these activities. Then agree on the most effective method.

ride a motorcycle
learn ballroom dancing
write a short story
use a new computer program
be a good public speaker
create, edit, and post videos

11 WORD POWER Personal qualities

A PAIR WORK How do we learn each of these things? Check (✓) your opinions.

	From parents	From school	On our own
artistic appreciation	☐	☐	☐
communication skills	☐	☐	☐
competitiveness	☐	☐	☐
concern for others	☐	☐	☐
cooperation	☐	☐	☐
courtesy	☐	☐	☐
creativity	☐	☐	☐
perseverance	☐	☐	☐
self-confidence	☐	☐	☐
tolerance	☐	☐	☐

B GROUP WORK How can you develop the personal qualities in part A? Use the activities in the box or your own ideas.

A: You can learn artistic appreciation by going to museums.
B: You can also learn it by studying painting or drawing.

> **some activities**
>
> studying world religions
> volunteering in a hospital
> taking a public speaking class
> performing in a play
> going to museums
> learning a martial art
> playing a team sport

12 WRITING Something I learned

A Think of a skill or a hobby you have learned. Read these questions and take notes. Then use your notes to write about what you learned.

What is required to be successful at it?
What are some ways people learn to do it?
How did you learn it?
What was difficult about learning it?

> I enjoy making jewelry, and many people say I am very talented at it. To make interesting jewelry, you need creativity. You have to use simple things and combine them in different ways to make beautiful pieces of jewelry.
>
> Some people learn to make jewelry by taking classes or by following instructions in a book. I first learned how to make a necklace by watching my aunt make . . .

B GROUP WORK Share your writing. Have any of your classmates' experiences inspired you to learn a new skill?

Learning Styles

Have you ever had trouble learning something? Did you overcome the problem? How?

Have you ever sat in class wondering if you would ever grasp the information that was being taught? Maybe the presentation didn't fit your learning style.

Our minds and bodies gather information in different ways and from all around us: seeing, hearing, and doing. Then our brains process that information, organizing it and making connections to things we already know. This process can also work in different ways: Do we think in pictures or words? Do we remember details or the big picture?

When we're trying to learn, it helps to know how our brain works. How do we best gather and organize information? Different people have different learning styles. For example, one person might struggle with written information but understand it immediately in an illustration. Another person might have problems with the picture, but not the written text.

Psychologists have identified seven basic learning styles:

Linguistic: These people learn by using language – listening, reading, speaking, and writing.
Logical: These people learn by applying formulas and scientific principles.
Visual: These people learn by seeing what they are learning.
Musical: Insted of finding music a distraction, these people learn well when information is presented through music.
Kinesthetic: Movement and physical activities help these people learn.
Intrapersonal: These people learn best if they associate new information directly with their own experiences.
Interpersonal: These people learn well by working with others.

You will often encounter situations that do not match your strongest learning style. If you know what your strengths are, you can develop strategies to balance your weaknesses for a more successful learning experience.

A Read the article. Find the words in *italics* in the article. Then match each word with its meaning.

.... 1. *grasp*	a. try hard to do something
.... 2. *gather*	b. understand
.... 3. *the big picture*	c. something that takes attention away
.... 4. *struggle*	d. show one thing is connected to another
.... 5. *distraction*	e. a general view of a situation
.... 6. *associate*	f. pick up or collect

B These sentences are false. Correct each one to make it true.

1. If you can't understand something, you aren't concentrating hard enough.
2. Linguistic learners will not comprehend written information.
3. A visual learner will probably learn best by listening and speaking.
4. A musical learner needs peace and quiet to focus on something.
5. Intrapersonal learners generally work well with other people.

C **GROUP WORK** Which learning styles do you think work best for you? Why?

Units 7–8 Progress check

SELF-ASSESSMENT

How well can you do these things? Check (✓) the boxes.

I can	Very well	OK	A little
Describe environmental problems (Ex. 1)	☐	☐	☐
Suggest solutions to problems (Ex. 2)	☐	☐	☐
Understand examples of personal qualities (Ex. 3)	☐	☐	☐
Ask about and express preferences (Ex. 4)	☐	☐	☐

 1 **GAME** *What's the cause?*

CLASS ACTIVITY Go around the room and make sentences. Check (✓) each phrase after it is used. The students who check the most items win.

EFFECT
- ☐ The quality of the air is being lowered
- ☐ Parks are being lost
- ☐ Water is being contaminated
- ☐ Landfills are overflowing
- ☐ Forests are being damaged
- ☐ City streets are being damaged

CAUSE
- ☐ heavy traffic
- ☐ acid rain
- ☐ overbuilding
- ☐ fumes from cars
- ☐ the lack of recycling
- ☐ factory waste

A: The quality of the air is being lowered . . .
B: . . . due to fumes from cars.

2 **DISCUSSION** *Social disasters*

A **PAIR WORK** Read these problems that friends sometimes have with each other. Suggest solutions for each problem.

A friend is having a party and you weren't invited.
Your roommate keeps damaging your things.
Your friend always keeps you on the phone too long.

useful expressions
One thing to do is to . . .
Another way to help is to . . .
The best thing to do is . . .

B **GROUP WORK** Agree on the best solution for each problem.

"One thing to do is to ask another friend to talk to your friend, to find out if it was a mistake."

3 LISTENING *I could just kick myself.*

▶ Listen to people talk about recent events and activities in their lives. What events and activities are they talking about? What quality does each person's behavior demonstrate? Complete the chart.

Event or activity	Quality	
1. Mark	☐ competitiveness	☐ cooperation
2. Joan	☐ perseverance	☐ tolerance
3. Kim	☐ self-confidence	☐ creativity

4 QUESTIONNAIRE *What works?*

A PAIR WORK Interview your partner. Circle the ways your partner prefers to improve his or her English.

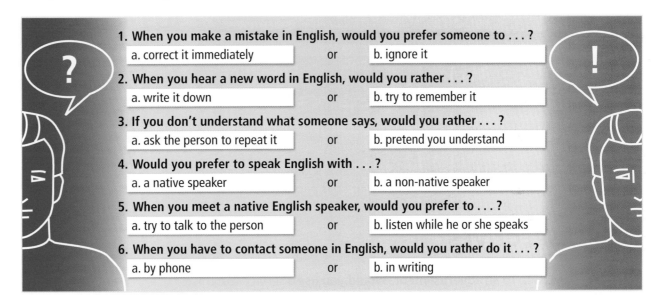

1. **When you make a mistake in English, would you prefer someone to . . . ?**
   a. correct it immediately   or   b. ignore it

2. **When you hear a new word in English, would you rather . . . ?**
   a. write it down   or   b. try to remember it

3. **If you don't understand what someone says, would you rather . . . ?**
   a. ask the person to repeat it   or   b. pretend you understand

4. **Would you prefer to speak English with . . . ?**
   a. a native speaker   or   b. a non-native speaker

5. **When you meet a native English speaker, would you prefer to . . . ?**
   a. try to talk to the person   or   b. listen while he or she speaks

6. **When you have to contact someone in English, would you rather do it . . . ?**
   a. by phone   or   b. in writing

"I'd prefer someone to correct my mistakes immediately."

B GROUP WORK Discuss the advantages and disadvantages of each option in part A. Are there better options for each situation?

A: When someone corrects me immediately, I get irritated.
B: Yes, but when someone ignores the mistake, you don't know that you've made one.
C: I think the best way someone can help you is by correcting you at the end of a conversation.

WHAT'S NEXT?

Look at your Self-assessment again. Do you need to review anything?

9 Improvements

1 SNAPSHOT

Nine commonly offered services

- Language tutoring ▷
- Computer services ▷
- House cleaning ▷
- Home repairs ▷
- Moving services ▷
- Financial services ▷
- Music lessons ▷
- Pet-sitting ▷
- Clothing alterations ▷

Source: Based on information from the community bulletin board at the Coffee Pot, New York City

Why would someone need these services? Have you ever used any of them?
What are some other common services and skills people offer?

2 PERSPECTIVES

A ◉ Listen to an advertisement. Would you use a service like this? Why or why not?

Hazel's Personal Services

Don't have time to do all the things you need to do? Call Hazel's Personal Services!

- Get your apartment cleaned.
- Have your car washed.
- Get your computer fixed.
- And much more . . . all for a very low price!

Call Hazel! (646) 555-2121
If Hazel doesn't offer the service you need, she'll find someone who does. Guaranteed!

Hazel offers:
- Computer support
- Repairs
- Beauty services
- Financial services
- Laundry and dry cleaning
- Pet-sitting

B What services do you need or want? What questions would you ask Hazel?

3 GRAMMAR FOCUS

Get or have something done ▶

Use get or have, the object, and the past participle of the verb to describe a service performed for you by someone else.

Do something yourself	Get/have something done for you
I **clean** my apartment every week.	I **get** my apartment **cleaned** (by Hazel) every week.
He **is washing** his car.	He **is having** his car **washed**.
They **fixed** their computer.	They **got** their computer **fixed**.
Did you **repair** your watch?	Did you **have** your watch **repaired**?
Where can I **print** these pictures?	Where can I **get** these pictures **printed**?

A Complete the sentences to express that the services are performed by someone else.

1. Luis didn't mow the lawn in front of his house. He _had it mowed_ . (have)
2. Samantha isn't cutting her own hair. She .... (get)
3. Barbara doesn't clean her apartment. She .... (have)
4. JoAnn and John didn't paint their house. They .... (get)
5. Doug isn't repairing his bike. He .... (have)

B PAIR WORK Take turns describing the services in the pictures.

| 1. Mei-ling | 2. Rodrigo | 3. Maggie | 4. Simon |

"Mei-ling is getting her skirt shortened."

C PAIR WORK Tell your partner about three things you've had done for you recently. Ask and answer questions for more information.

4 PRONUNCIATION *Sentence stress*

A ▶ Listen and practice. Notice that when the object becomes a pronoun (sentence B), it is no longer stressed.

A: Where can I get my **watch fixed**?

A: Where can I have my **shoes shined**?

B: You can get it **fixed** at the **Time** Shop.

B: You can have them **shined** at **Sunshine** Shoes.

B GROUP WORK Ask questions about three things you want to have done. Pay attention to sentence stress. Other students give answers.

5 DISCUSSION *Different places, different ways*

GROUP WORK Are these services available in your country? For those that aren't, do you think they would be a good idea?

Can you . . . ?

have your portrait drawn by a street artist
get your blood pressure checked at a pharmacy
have your clothes dry-cleaned at work
get library books delivered to your home
have your shoes shined on the street
get your car washed for less than $15
have a suit made in under 24 hours
get your teeth whitened
have pizza delivered after midnight

A: Can you have your portrait drawn by a street artist?
B: Sure! You can have it done at . . .

6 INTERCHANGE 9 *Put yourself in my shoes!*

What do teenagers worry about? Go to Interchange 9 on page 123.

7 WORD POWER *Three-word phrasal verbs*

A Match each phrasal verb in these sentences with its meaning. Then compare with a partner.

Phrasal verbs

1. Jennifer has **broken up with** her boyfriend – again! ....
2. Kevin **came up with** a great idea for our class reunion. ....
3. I'm not **looking forward to** watching my neighbor's dogs. They're not very friendly. ....
4. My doctor says I'm overweight. I should **cut down on** fatty foods. ....
5. Rob can't **keep up with** the students in his Mandarin class. He should get a tutor. ....
6. I can't **put up with** the noise on my street! I'll have to move. ....
7. My girlfriend doesn't **get along with** her roommate. They're always fighting. ....
8. Bill can't **take care of** his own finances. He has an accountant manage his money. ....

Meanings

a. be excited for
b. end a romantic relationship with
c. stay in pace with
d. tolerate
e. reduce the quantity of
f. have a good relationship with
g. be responsible for
h. think of; develop

B **PAIR WORK** Take turns making sentences with each phrasal verb in part A.

8 CONVERSATION *I have two left feet!*

A ▶ Listen and practice.

James: This is so depressing! I haven't had a date since Angela broke up with me. What can I do?

Mike: Why don't you join an online dating service? That's how I met Amy.

James: Actually, I've tried that. But the people you meet are always different from what you expect.

Mike: Well, what about taking a dance class? A friend of mine met his wife that way.

James: A dance class? Are you serious?

Mike: Sure, why not? They offer them here at the gym.

James: I don't think that's a very good idea. Have you ever seen me dance? I have two left feet!

B CLASS ACTIVITY   What are some other good ways to meet people?

9 GRAMMAR FOCUS

> ### Making suggestions ▶
>
> **With modals + verbs**
> **Maybe you could go** to a chat room.
>
> **With gerunds**
> **What about taking** a dance class?
> **Have you thought about asking** your friends to introduce you to their other friends?
>
> **With negative questions**
> **Why don't you join** an online dating service?
>
> **With infinitives**
> **One option is to join** a club.
> **It might be a good idea to check out** those discussion groups at the bookstore.

A Circle the correct answers. Then practice with a partner.

1. A: How can I build self-confidence?
   B: **What about / Why don't you** participating in more social activities?

2. A: What could help me be happier?
   B: **Maybe / One option** you could try not to get annoyed about little things.

3. A: How can I get better grades?
   B: **Have you thought about / It might be a good idea** to join a study group.

4. A: What can I do to save money?
   B: **Why don't you / What about** come up with a budget?

5. A: How can I get along with my roommate better?
   B: **Why don't you / Have you thought about** planning fun activities to look forward to every week?

B GROUP WORK   Take turns asking and answering the questions in part A. Answer with your own suggestions.

10 LISTENING All you have to do is . . .

A ▶ Listen to people give different suggestions for each problem. Put a line through the suggestion that was *not* given.

1. How to overcome shyness:
   a. read a self-help book
   b. join a club
   c. see a therapist
   d. take medication

2. How to stop biting your fingernails:
   a. count instead
   b. wear gloves
   c. paint your nails
   d. figure out why you're nervous

3. How to organize your busy schedule:
   a. program your phone
   b. make a list of priorities
   c. cancel appointments
   d. talk to a consultant

B PAIR WORK Look at the suggestions. Which one seems the most helpful? Why?

11 SPEAKING Bad habits

GROUP WORK Make three suggestions for how to break each of these bad habits. Then share your ideas with the class. Which ideas are the most creative?

How can I stop . . . ?

buying things I don't need

eating junk food at night

cracking my knuckles

"One thing you could do is cut up your credit cards. And why don't you . . . ?"

12 WRITING A letter of advice

A Imagine you are an advice columnist at a magazine. Choose one of the letters below and make a list of suggestions. Then write a reply.

My best friend seems anxious a lot. She bites her fingernails and always looks tired. I don't think she's eating right, either. How can I convince her to take better care of herself?
– *Worried*

I argue with my girlfriend all the time. I try to do nice things for her, but we always end up in a fight. I can't put up with this much longer – what can I do?
– *Frustrated*

B GROUP WORK Take turns reading your advice. Whose advice do you think will work? Why?

Critical Thinking

Have you ever said something – and then regretted that you didn't think carefully before opening your mouth? What happened?

1 "Think before you speak!" Has anyone ever said that to you? It's only human to react quickly and perhaps emotionally to things that happen. But without giving ourselves sufficient thinking time, we may see things in terms of black and white instead of considering various shades of gray or other colors. Also, it's all too easy to ignore connections and consequences.

2 At one level, thinking is fairly simple. For instance, it might simply involve making a shopping list. However, there is a deeper and more complex level of thinking. This is often called "critical thinking," and it has several characteristics. First, it requires that you rely on reason rather than emotion. This means you have to look objectively at all available

evidence and decide if it is true, false, or perhaps partly true. Second, you have to be self-aware and recognize your biases and prejudices because these may cause you to think subjectively. A third characteristic is that you need to be open to new ideas and interpretations.

3 Critical thinking can help you in just about everything you do. One of the most important things it helps you do is solve problems. This has always been an asset in many traditional fields, such as education, research, business and management. But it's also very useful to help people keep up with the new, fast-moving knowledge economy, which is driven by information and technology. Modern workers often have to analyze and integrate information from many different sources in order to solve problems.

4 We all sometimes speak before we think, and we all have blind spots. Nevertheless, while thinking critically doesn't always happen automatically, it will certainly serve you well whatever you do in life.

A Read the article. Then write the number of each paragraph next to its main idea.

.... For many people, critical thinking is useful in the workplace.
.... It's worth the effort to think critically.
.... We often don't allow ourselves enough time to think.
.... Critical thinking has three important aspects.

B Read about these people. Which of the three characteristics of critical thinking did they need to apply? Explain your answers.

a = Check if the evidence is true.   b = Recognize your prejudices.   c = Be open to new ideas.

.... 1. Jane worked as a bank teller for ten years. She never considered doing anything else. When she was offered a promotion, she refused it.
.... 2. Bella received an email from someone she didn't know. The email said she had won $1 million in the lottery. She immediately bought a new car.
.... 3. Ian thinks our new neighbors are loud, but I disagree. I think he's just more sensitive to the noise because they play music and watch TV shows that aren't in English.

C **GROUP WORK** How good are you at critical thinking? How has it helped you?

10 The past and the future

1 SNAPSHOT

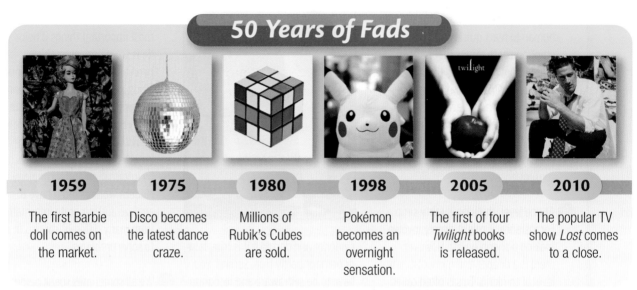

50 Years of Fads

1959	1975	1980	1998	2005	2010
The first Barbie doll comes on the market.	Disco becomes the latest dance craze.	Millions of Rubik's Cubes are sold.	Pokémon becomes an overnight sensation.	The first of four *Twilight* books is released.	The popular TV show *Lost* comes to a close.

Sources: *New York Public Library Book of Chronologies;* http://answers.yahoo.com

Have any of these fads ever been popular in your country?
Can you think of four other fads from the past or present?
Is there anything popular right now that could be a fad?

2 CONVERSATION *I'm good at history.*

A ▶ Listen and practice.

Emma: Look. Here's a quiz on events of the twentieth century.
Steve: Oh, let me give it a try. I'm good at history.
Emma: All right. First question: When did World War I begin?
Steve: I think it began in 1917.
Emma: Huh. And how long has the United Nations been in existence?
Steve: Uh, since Kennedy became president in 1961.
Emma: Hmm. Next question: How long were the Beatles together?
Steve: Well, they started in 1965, and broke up in 1980, so they were together for 15 years. So, how am I doing so far?
Emma: Not very well. Not one of your answers is correct!

B ▶ Do you know the answers to the three questions in part A? Listen to the rest of the conversation. What are the correct answers?

3 GRAMMAR FOCUS

Referring to time in the past ▶

A point or period of time in the past

When did World War II take place?
During the 1940s. **In** the 1940s. Over 70 years **ago**.

How long were the Beatles together?
From 1960 **to** 1970. **For** ten years.

A period of time that continues into the present

How long has the United Nations been in existence?
Since 1945. **Since** World War II ended. **For** about the last 70 years.

A Complete the paragraphs with the **boldface** words from the grammar box. Then compare with a partner.

1. The planet Pluto was discovered .... 1930. Scientists accepted this .... many years but .... the 1970s, some began to question if Pluto was indeed a planet. .... 2008, after a long debate, Pluto was downgraded to a new category called "dwarf planet." .... that time, our solar system has had only eight planets.

2. Scientists found a new species of dinosaur in the U.S. state of Utah .... 2007. Like some other species of dinosaur, it ate plants. Unlike other species, however, it had 15 giant horns on its head. These dinosaurs lived .... over 30 million years .... the Cretaceous period. Scientists believe they lived .... about 68 .... 99 million years ....

B GROUP WORK Write two true and two false statements about world events. Then take turns reading your statements. Others give correct information for the false statements.

A: Bill Clinton was president of the U.S. for four years.
B: That's false. He was president for eight years.

4 PRONUNCIATION Syllable stress

A ▶ Listen and practice. Notice which syllable has the main stress in these four- and five-syllable words. Notice the secondary stress.

○ ● ○○	○ ○ ● ○	○ ○ ○○● ○
identify	disadvantage	communication

appreciate
assassination
catastrophe
consideration
conversation
revolution

....

....

B ▶ Listen to the words in the box. Which syllable has the main stress? Write the words in the correct column in part A.

5 WORD POWER Historic events

A Match each word with the best example. Then compare with a partner.

1. achievement ....
2. assassination ....
3. discovery ....
4. election ....
5. epidemic ....
6. natural disaster ....
7. revolution ....
8. terrorist act ....

a. The eruption of Mount St. Helens in 1980 destroyed over 250 homes.
b. In the late 18th century, 13 American colonies broke free of British rule.
c. Four planes were hijacked in the United States on September 11, 2001.
d. In 2003, a dinosaur with feathers and four wings was found in China.
e. Since the late 1970s, HIV has infected more than 60 million people.
f. In 2008, Barack Obama beat John McCain to become U.S. president.
g. U.S. president John F. Kennedy was shot to death in 1963.
h. In 1953, Sir Edmund Hillary and the Sherpa Tenzing Norgay were the first to reach the summit of Mount Everest.

B PAIR WORK Give another example for each kind of historic event in part A.

"The exploration of Mars is an amazing achievement."

6 DISCUSSION It made a difference.

GROUP WORK Choose two or three historic events (an election, an epidemic, an achievement, etc.) that had an impact on your country. Discuss the questions.

What happened (or what was achieved)? When did it happen?
What was the immediate effect on your country? the world? your family?
Did it change things permanently? How is life different now?

"Recently a large oil field was discovered off the coast of Brazil. . . ."

7 WRITING A biography

A Find information about a person who has had a major influence on the world or your country. Answer these questions. Then write a biography.

What is this person famous for?
How and when did he or she become famous?
What are his or her important achievements?

B PAIR WORK Exchange biographies. What additional details can your partner add?

Kim Dae-jung (1925–2009)

Kim Dae-jung became famous during the 1960s, when he was first elected to government. He became an opposition leader and spent many years in the 1970s and 1980s in prison.

He was president of South Korea from 1998 to 2003. He was awarded the Nobel Peace Prize in 2000 for his efforts toward peace, democracy, and human rights. Kim Dae-jung died . . .

8 INTERCHANGE 10 History buff

Find out how good you are at history.
Student A, go to Interchange 10A on page 124; Student B, go to Interchange 10B on page 126.

9 PERSPECTIVES

A 🔊 Listen to a survey about the future. Check (✓) the predictions you think will happen.

What will the future hold?

☐ Computers will recognize any voice command. You won't need a keyboard.

☐ Within 20 years, scientists will have discovered a cure for baldness.

☐ People will be living in cities under the ocean.

☐ By 2025, world leaders will have eliminated terrorism.

☐ Robots will be performing most factory jobs.

☐ By 2050, we will have set up human communities on Mars.

☐ Medical scientists will find a cure for Alzheimer's disease.

B Which of the predictions do you think will affect you?

10 GRAMMAR FOCUS

> ### Predicting the future with will 🔊
>
> *Use will to predict future events or situations.*
> Computers **will recognize** any voice command. You **won't need** a keyboard.
>
> *Use future continuous to predict ongoing actions.*
> People **will be living** in cities under the ocean.
>
> *Use future perfect to predict actions that will be completed by a certain time.*
> Within 20 years, scientists **will have discovered** a cure for baldness.
> By 2050, we **will have set up** human communities on Mars.

A Complete these predictions with the correct verb forms. (More than one answer is possible.) Then compare with a partner.

1. In ten years, flights from New York to Tokyo .... (take) less than two hours.
2. Soon, they .... (sell) computers that can translate perfectly from one language to another.
3. By the middle of the twenty-first century, scientists .... (discover) a way to prevent aging.
4. Sometime in the future, scientists .... (invent) a machine that transmits our thoughts.
5. In the future, people .... (live) on the moon.
6. In less than a decade, the polar ice caps .... (melt), and many islands .... (disappear).

B GROUP WORK Discuss each prediction in part A. Do you agree or disagree?

A: In ten years, flights from New York to Tokyo will take less than two hours. What do you think?
B: Oh, I totally agree. I think they'll use space-shuttle technology to build faster airplanes.
C: I'm not so sure. Those flights normally take about 14 hours. How are they going to come up with an invention that shortens the trip by 12 hours?

C CLASS ACTIVITY Discuss these questions.

1. What three recently developed technologies will have the greatest impact on our lives in the next 20 years?
2. What are the three most important changes that will have occurred on earth by 2050?
3. Which three jobs will people *not* be doing in 50 years? Why?

11 LISTENING *A perfect future?*

A ▶ Listen to people discuss changes that will affect these topics of interest in the future. Write down two changes for each topic.

Future changes		
1. work	....	....
2. transportation	....	....
3. education	....	....
4. health	....	....

B GROUP WORK Can you suggest one more possible change for each topic?

12 DISCUSSION *Things will be different!*

GROUP WORK Talk about these questions.

What do you think you'll be doing a year from now? five years from now?
Do you think you'll still be living in the same place?
What are three things you think you'll have accomplished within the next five years?
What are three things you won't have done within the next five years?
In what ways do you think you'll have changed by the time you retire?

Food Trends National.com

HOME | **FOOD TRUCKS** | RESTAURANTS | FAST FOOD | CATERERS

 Tweet to eat

Chef Roy Choi of Kogi BBQ

Skim the article. What's innovative about Kogi BBQ's business model?

As technology evolves, new business models emerge. For many years, businesses have sold their products and services online, but now social networking is changing the way people do business. Kogi BBQ in Los Angeles has found profitable ways to make the most of today's technology.

Kogi BBQ is a restaurant that serves a fusion of Korean and Mexican food concocted by Chef Roy Choi. The kimchi quesadilla and short rib taco are two favorites. Besides its menu, Kogi BBQ is different from other restaurants because people don't come to it; it goes to the people. Kogi BBQ uses five food-service trucks called Azul, Verde, Roja, Naranja, and Rosita to deliver cheap, gourmet fast food to long lines of hungry – and mostly young – customers throughout the city.

But how do people know where to find a Kogi BBQ truck? Technology is at the center of its business. Kogi BBQ uses the social networking site Twitter to inform customers where each of its trucks will be and when. The tweets (Twitter messages) look like this one:

Dinner time: Azul 6 PM - 9 PM @ Northridge (Devonshire and Reseda);
10:30 PM - 11:30 PM @ City of Industry (18558 Gale Ave.)

Customers can even post requests, like this one:

Can you come to Colima in Rowland Heights earlier? Maybe around 6-9? Thanks.

Kogi BBQ has been a viral sensation in Los Angeles. In addition to Twitter, Kogi BBQ uses YouTube, Facebook, blogs, and other electronic tools, like text messaging, to stay connected with its customers. By avoiding traditional advertising and building its business around an online community, Kogi BBQ has created a "Kogi Kulture," fueled by dedicated fans eager to spread the word.

Time will tell if this is a passing fad or the wave of the future. Either way, this much is true: As technology changes, businesses will figure out how to capitalize on it.

A Read the article. Then complete the summary with information from the article.

.... impacts the way people do .... Kogi BBQ, a trendy restaurant in Los Angeles, has developed a successful business .... based on new technology. Kogi BBQ delivers gourmet fast food from five .... To inform customers of their whereabouts, Kogi BBQ uses .... sites, like Twitter. In so doing, Kogi BBQ has built an online .... of enthusiastic customers who love and seek out its food.

B Use information in the article to answer the following questions in your own words.

1. Where does Kogi BBQ do business?
2. Why is Kogi BBQ considered fusion cuisine?
3. What is unique about Kogi BBQ?
4. What is a tweet?
5. What is "Kogi Kulture"?
6. What does it mean to *capitalize on* something?

C GROUP WORK What other companies use social networking to enhance their business? How might technology change the way people do business in the future?

Units 9–10 Progress check

SELF-ASSESSMENT

How well can you do these things? Check (✓) the boxes.

I can	Very well	OK	A little
Describe experiences of getting/having things done (Ex. 1)	☐	☐	☐
Ask for and give advice about problems (Ex. 2)	☐	☐	☐
Understand and give descriptions of historical events (Ex. 3)	☐	☐	☐
Make predictions about the future (Ex. 4)	☐	☐	☐

1 DISCUSSION *Once in a while*

GROUP WORK Take turns asking questions about these services. When someone answers "yes," find out why and when the service was performed, and who performed it.

have your photo taken professionally
get your apartment painted
get your eyes checked
have your home redecorated or remodeled
get something translated

A: Have any of you ever had your photo taken professionally?
B: Yes, I have. I had one taken a few months ago.
C: Really? Why did you have it taken? . . .

have a photo taken

2 ROLE PLAY *A friend in need*

Student A: Choose one of these problems. Decide on the details of the problem. Then tell your partner about it and get some advice.

I'm looking forward to my vacation, but I haven't saved enough money.
I don't get along with my . . . . We're always fighting.
I can't take care of my pet anymore. I don't know what to do.

Student B: Your partner tells you about a problem. Ask questions about it. Then consider the situation and offer two pieces of advice.

Change roles and choose another situation.

useful expressions
Have you thought about . . . ?
It might be a good idea to . . .
Maybe you could . . .
Why don't you . . . ?

3 LISTENING *How good is your history?*

A ▶ Listen to people discuss the questions. Write the correct answers.

1. When was the first Iditarod? ....
2. How long did apartheid exist in South Africa? ....
3. When did a spacecraft first land on Mars? ....
4. How long was the Berlin Wall up? ....
5. How long have the modern Olympics existed? ....

B **GROUP WORK** Write three more questions about historic events. (Make sure you know the answers.) Then take turns asking your questions. Who has the most correct answers?

4 SURVEY *Five years from now, . . .*

A **CLASS ACTIVITY** How many of your classmates will have done these things in the next five years? Write down the number of "yes" and "no" answers. When someone answers "yes," ask follow-up questions.

	"Yes" answers	"No" answers
1. move to a new city	....	....
2. get a (new) job	....	....
3. have a(nother) child	....	....
4. travel abroad	....	....
5. learn another language	....	....
6. get a college or master's degree	....	....

A: Five years from now, will you have moved to a new city?
B: Yes, I think I will have moved away from here.
A: Where do you think you'll move to?
B: I'd like to live in Shanghai.
A: Really? What will you be doing there?

Shanghai

B **GROUP WORK** Tally the results of the survey as a group. Then take turns telling the class any additional information you found out.

"Very few people think they will have moved to a new city in five years. Only two people think that they will move. One person thinks he'll move to Shanghai, and one person thinks she'll move to Boston."

WHAT'S NEXT

Look at your Self-assessment again. Do you need to review anything?

11 Life's little lessons

1 SNAPSHOT

Rites of Passage
Some important life events

- First birthday (or first 100 days, as in South Korea)
- First haircut
- Losing your first tooth
- First day of school
- Sweet 16 (or Sweet 15, as in Latin America)
- First job

- High school graduation
- 20th birthday (or 21st birthday, as in the United States and Canada)
- College graduation
- Marriage
- Becoming a parent
- Retirement

Source: *Peace Corps Handbook for RPCV Speakers*

Which rites of passage, or life events, are important in your country?
   Check (✓) the events.
What are other rites of passage for people in your country?
Have any of these things recently happened to you or someone you know?

2 CONVERSATION *I was really immature.*

A ▶ Listen and practice.

Alan: So what were you like when you were younger?
Carol: When I was a kid, I was kind of irresponsible.
Alan: You? Really? What made you change?
Carol: Graduating from high school.
Alan: What do you mean?
Carol: Well, until I graduated, I'd never had any important responsibilities. But then, I went off to college. . . .
Alan: I know what you mean. I was really immature when I was a teenager.
Carol: So what made *you* change?
Alan: I think I became more mature after I got my first job and moved away from home. Once I had a job, I became totally independent.
Carol: Where did you work?
Alan: I worked for my dad at the bank.

B ▶ Listen to the rest of the conversation.
What was another turning point for Carol? for Alan?

Time clauses ▶

Before I had my first job, I was really immature.
After I got my first job, I became more mature.
Once I had a job, I became totally independent.
The moment I moved away from home, I felt like a different person.
As soon as I got my own bank account, I started to be more responsible.
Until I graduated, I'd never had any important responsibilities.
By the time I graduated from high school, I had already started working.

A Match the clauses in column A with appropriate information in column B.
Then compare with a partner.

A

1. By the time I was 15, ...
2. Until I started working part-time, ...
3. The moment I got my first paycheck, ...
4. As soon as I left home, ...
5. Once I started sharing an apartment, ...
6. After I began a relationship, ...
7. Before I traveled abroad, ...
8. Until I got really sick, ...

B

a. I didn't appreciate my own country.
b. I began to understand the value of money.
c. I learned that love can hurt!
d. I realized that I wasn't a child anymore.
e. I had learned how to take care of myself.
f. I learned how to get along better with people.
g. I had never saved any money.
h. I hadn't understood the importance of
   good health.

B Which of the clauses in column A can you relate to your life?
Add your own information to those clauses. Then compare with a partner.

"The moment I got my first paycheck, I became more independent."

C **GROUP WORK** What do you think people learn from these events? Write sentences
using time clauses in the present. Then take turns reading and talking about them.

1. getting a credit card
2. going out on your first date
3. getting your first job
4. getting your driver's license
5. buying your first bike, moped, or car
6. opening your own bank account
7. getting married
8. becoming a parent

1. Once you get a credit card, you learn
it's important not to overspend.

4 LISTENING *Important events*

A ▶ Listen to three people describe important events in their lives. Complete the chart.

	Event	How it affected him or her
1. Sally	....	....
2. Henry	....	....
3. Debbie	....	....

B ▶ Listen again. What do these three people have in common?

5 SPEAKING *Milestones*

A **PAIR WORK** In your country, how old are people when these things happen?

get a driver's license   graduate from college
begin to date   get married
move out of their parents' home   retire

B **GROUP WORK** Choose three milestones. What do you think life is like before and after each one? Join another pair and discuss.

"Before people get a driver's license, they are very dependent on their parents. Once they get a license, they . . . "

6 WORD POWER *Behavior and personality*

A **PAIR WORK** At what age do you think people possess these traits? Check (✓) one or more ages for each trait.

	In their teens	In their 20s	In their 30s	In their 40s	In their 60s
ambitious	☐	☐	☐	☐	☐
argumentative	☐	☐	☐	☐	☐
carefree	☐	☐	☐	☐	☐
conscientious	☐	☐	☐	☐	☐
naive	☐	☐	☐	☐	☐
pragmatic	☐	☐	☐	☐	☐
rebellious	☐	☐	☐	☐	☐
sensible	☐	☐	☐	☐	☐
sophisticated	☐	☐	☐	☐	☐

B **GROUP WORK** Use the words in part A to describe people you know.

"My older brother is argumentative. He disagrees with me about everything!"

7 PERSPECTIVES *I should have . . .*

A ▶ Listen to Maya Misery talk about her regrets. Do you have any similar regrets?

"I should have studied something more practical while I was in college."

"If I'd listened to my mother, I would have learned to play a musical instrument."

"If I'd been more ambitious in college, I could have learned to speak another language."

"I shouldn't have waited so long to choose a major."

"If I hadn't wasted so much money last year, I would have moved into my own apartment by now."

"If I hadn't been so irresponsible, I could have gotten better grades."

B What do you suggest to help Maya feel better?

8 GRAMMAR FOCUS

Expressing regret and describing hypothetical situations ▶

Use should have + the past participle to express regret.
I should have studied something more practical when I was in college.
I shouldn't have waited so long to choose a major.

Use would have + the past participle to express probable outcomes in hypothetical situations.
Use could have + the past participle to express possible outcomes.
If **I'd listened** to my mother, I **would have learned** to play a musical instrument.
If I **hadn't been** so irresponsible, I **could have gotten** better grades.

A For each statement, write a sentence expressing regret. Then talk with a partner about which statements are true for you.

1. I was very rebellious when I was younger.
2. I didn't pay attention to what I ate as a kid.
3. I didn't make many friends in high school.
4. I was very argumentative as a teenager.
5. I was too naive when I started looking for my first job.

> 1. I should have been less rebellious when I was younger.

B Match the clauses in column A with appropriate information in column B.

A
1. If I'd listened to my parents, ...
2. If I'd been more active, ...
3. If I'd been more ambitious, ...
4. If I'd studied harder in school, ...
5. If I'd saved my money, ...

B
a. I wouldn't have had to borrow so much.
b. I could have learned a lot more.
c. I would have made more pragmatic decisions.
d. I wouldn't have gained all this weight.
e. I could have gotten a promotion.

C Add your own information to the clauses in column A. Then compare in groups.

9 INTERCHANGE 11 *When I was younger, . . .*

Imagine if things were different. Go to Interchange 11 on page 125.

10 PRONUNCIATION *Reduction of* **have** *and* **been**

A ▶ Listen and practice. Notice how **have** and **been** are reduced in these sentences.

I should **have been** less selfish when I was younger.
If I'd **been** more ambitious, I could **have** gotten a promotion.

B PAIR WORK Complete these sentences and practice them. Pay attention
to the reduced forms of **have** and **been**.

I should have been . . . when I was younger.   If I'd been more . . . , I could have . . .
I should have been . . . in high school.   If I'd been less . . . , I would have . . .

11 LISTENING *Regrets*

A ▶ Listen to people describe their regrets. What does each person regret?

	What does he or she regret?	Why does he or she regret it?
1. Alex	....	....
2. Yi-yun	....	....
3. Jacob	....	....

B ▶ Listen again. Why does he or she regret it?

12 WRITING *A letter of apology*

A Think about something you regret doing that you want to apologize for.
Consider the questions below. Then write a letter of apology.

What did you do? What were the consequences?
Is there any way you can undo those consequences?

> Dear Jonathan,
>   I'm really sorry I forgot to tell you that my party
> was canceled. You worked so hard making all those cookies!
> I should've called or sent you a text before you started
> baking them, but I got really busy at work and didn't
> get around to it. If I'd been more conscientious, . . .

B PAIR WORK Read your partner's letter. Talk about
what you would have done if you'd had a similar regret.

Milestones Around the World

Scan the article. Where does each milestone take place? Who is each milestone for?

EGYPT

In Egypt, many families with new babies celebrate *El Sebou'*, which means *the seventh*. Some say the ancient pharaohs believed that children who lived to be seven days old were ready for a long and healthy life. Family and friends meet at the parents' house, and the baby is put in a round wooden cradle called a *ghorbal*. Songs are sung, and the baby is rocked gently to awaken its senses. Salt is scattered to keep evil away, and the mother carries the baby around the house. Children follow with lit candles. Finally, bags full of candies, sweets, and gold- and silver-like coins are distributed to all attendees.

MEXICO

Families in Mexico and several other Latin American countries have a special celebration for *La quinceañera*, the birthday girl who turns 15 years old. It marks a girl's passage from girlhood to womanhood. Wearing a spectacular dress and carrying a bouquet of flowers, the girl arrives at a church for a thanksgiving service. Then there is a party with live music, dancing, and plenty of delicious food. An important moment is when the girl cuts a multilayered birthday cake.

VANUATU

On a single island in the South Pacific nation of Vanuatu, young men hurl themselves from a 30-meter wooden tower, with only vines tied around their ankles to break their fall. The original bungee jumpers, these "land divers" jump to prove their manhood. The goal is for the young man's shoulder to just touch the ground. The vines' measurement must be exact as there is no safety net. When a young man jumps, his mother holds a favorite childhood item. After the jump, she throws the item away, demonstrating that he is now a man.

A Read the article. Find the words in *italics* in the article. Then match each word with its meaning.

.... 1. *senses*   a. thrown in different directions
.... 2. *scattered*   b. demonstrate
.... 3. *spectacular*   c. throw
.... 4. *plenty*   d. sight, hearing, taste, touch, and smell
.... 5. *hurl*   e. very exciting to look at
.... 6. *prove*   f. more than enough

B Check (✓) the correct milestone(s) for each description.

	El Sebou'	La quinceañera	Land diving
1. The person's family participates.	☐	☐	☐
2. There is a religious ceremony.	☐	☐	☐
3. Children carry candles.	☐	☐	☐
4. The event is dangerous.	☐	☐	☐
5. The event requires special clothing.	☐	☐	☐

C **GROUP WORK** Which of the milestones do you think is the most serious? Which is the most fun? Why do you think people celebrate milestones like these?

The right stuff

SUCCESS STORIES

Five of the world's most successful businesses

COMPANY	MAIN PRODUCTS	FACT
Coca-Cola	soft drinks, juice, and bottled water	Coca-Cola is the best-known English word in the world after *OK*.
Sony	electronics equipment, movies, and TVs	Some early products included tape recorders and rice cookers.
Levi Strauss	jeans and casual clothing	The first jeans were made for men looking for gold in California.
Google	Internet-based products and services	Google comes from *googol*, which is the math term for the number 1 followed by 100 zeros.
Nestlé	chocolate, instant coffee, and bottled water	Nestlé means *little nest*, which symbolizes security and family.

Sources: *Hoover's Handbook of American Business 2003*; www.sony.net; www.google.com; www.nestle.com

Which of these products exist in your country? Are they successful?
Can you think of three successful companies in your country? What do they produce?

2 PERSPECTIVES

A ● Listen to the survey. What makes a business successful?
Number the choices from 1 (most important) to 3 (least important).

What makes a business successful?

☐ **1** Most important
☐ **2** Somewhat important
☐ **3** Least important

1. In order for a language school to succeed, it has to have
   ☐ a variety of classes ☐ a convenient location ☐ inexpensive courses

2. To run a popular Internet café, it's a good idea to have
   ☐ plenty of computers ☐ good snacks and drinks ☐ a fast connection

3. In order to operate a successful movie theater, it has to have
   ☐ the latest movies ☐ good snacks and drinks ☐ big screens

4. To establish a trendy restaurant, it's important to have
   ☐ fashionable servers ☐ delicious food ☐ good music

5. For an athletic center to be profitable, it needs to have
   ☐ good trainers ☐ modern exercise equipment ☐ a variety of classes

6. For a concert hall to be successful, it should have
   ☐ excellent acoustics ☐ comfortable seats ☐ affordable tickets

B **GROUP WORK** Compare your answers. Do you agree on the most important success factors?

3 PRONUNCIATION Reduced words

A ▶ Listen and practice. Notice how certain words are reduced in conversation.

In order **for** a café **to** succeed, it needs **to** have good food **and** service.
For an airline **to** be successful, it has **to** maintain a good safety record.

B PAIR WORK Take turns reading the sentences in Exercise 2 aloud. Use your first choice to complete each sentence. Pay attention to reduced words.

4 GRAMMAR FOCUS

Describing purpose ▶

Infinitive clauses

To run a popular Internet café,	it's a good idea to have plenty of computers.
(In order) to establish a trendy restaurant,	it's important to have fashionable servers.

Infinitive clauses with for

For an athletic center **to be** profitable,	it needs to have modern exercise equipment.
(In order) for a language school **to succeed**,	it has to have a convenient location.

A Match each goal with a suggestion. Then practice the sentences with a partner.

Goals

1. For a health club to attract new people, ...
2. In order to run a profitable restaurant, ...
3. To establish a successful dance club, ...
4. For a coffee bar to succeed, ...
5. To run a successful clothing boutique, ...

Suggestions

a. you need to hire a talented chef.
b. it's a good idea to offer desserts, too.
c. you need to keep up with the latest styles.
d. it needs to have great music and lighting.
e. it has to offer the latest equipment.

B PAIR WORK Give another suggestion for each goal in part A.

C GROUP WORK Look at the picture of a coffee shop. For it to stay in business, what should be done?

"For this coffee shop to stay in business, it needs . . ."

5 WORD POWER *Qualities for success*

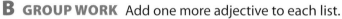

A PAIR WORK What qualities are important for success?
Rank them from 1 to 5.

A model	**A salesperson**	**A magazine**
☐ fashionable	☐ clever	☐ affordable
☐ gorgeous	☐ charming	☐ attractive
☐ industrious	☐ knowledgeable	☐ entertaining
☐ muscular	☐ persuasive	☐ informative
☐ slender	☐ tough	☐ well written

B GROUP WORK Add one more adjective to each list.

"For a model to be successful, he or she needs to be . . ."

6 ROLE PLAY *You're hired!*

Student A: Interview two people for one of these jobs. What qualities do they need for success? Decide who is more qualified for the job.

Students B and C: You are applying for the same job. What are your best qualities? Convince the interviewer that you are more qualified for the job.

host for a political talk show   server at a trendy café   exercise equipment salesperson

A: To be a good host for a political talk show, you need to be knowledgeable. Are you?
B: Yes. I follow politics closely, and I'm also tough. I'm not afraid to ask hard questions.
C: I'm fascinated by politics, and I'm industrious, so I would do thorough research.

7 CONVERSATION *I thought you'd never ask!*

A ▶ Listen and practice.

Mayumi: What's your favorite club, Ben?
    Ben: The Soul Club. They have fabulous music, and it's never crowded, so it's easy to get in.
Mayumi: That's funny. There's always a long wait outside my favorite club. I like it because it's always packed.
    Ben: Why do you think it's so popular?
Mayumi: Well, it just opened a few months ago, everything is brand-new and modern, and lots of fashionable people go there. It's called the Casablanca.
    Ben: Oh, right! I hear the reason people go there is just to be seen.
Mayumi: Exactly! Do you want to go some night?
    Ben: I thought you'd never ask!

B CLASS ACTIVITY What are some popular places in your city?
Do you ever go to any of these places? Why or why not?

Giving reasons ▶

I like the Casablanca **because** it's always packed.
Since it's always so packed, there's a long wait outside the club.
It's popular **because of** the fashionable people.
The Soul Club is famous **for** its fantastic music.
Due to the crowds, the Casablanca is difficult to get in to.
The reason (**that/why**) people go there **is** just to be seen.

A Complete the paragraph with *because, since, because of, for, due to*, and *the reason*. Then compare with a partner. (More than one answer is possible.)

MTV is one of the most popular television networks in the world. People love MTV not only .... its music videos, but also .... its clever and diverse programming. .... it keeps its shows up-to-the-minute, young people watch MTV for the latest fads in music and fashion. MTV is also well known .... its music awards show. .... so many people watch it is to see all the fashionable guests. MTV even has reality shows. These shows are popular .... they appeal to young people. .... MTV's widespread popularity, many teenagers have become less industrious with their homework!

B What reason explains the success of each situation? (More than one answer is possible.) Compare ideas with a partner.

Situation

1. Nokia is a successful company ....
2. People love Levi's jeans ....
3. The BBC is well known ....
4. Huge supermarket chains are popular ....
5. People everywhere drink Coca-Cola ....
6. Apple products are famous ....
7. Nike is a popular brand of clothing ....
8. Many people like megastores ....

Reason

a. since prices are generally more affordable.
b. due to its ever-changing product line.
c. because they have always been fashionable.
d. for their innovative designs.
e. because of its informative programming.
f. for their big choice of products.
g. since it advertises worldwide.
h. because the advertising is clever and entertaining.

C **PAIR WORK** Suggest two more reasons for each success in part B.

A: Nokia is a successful company because its commercials are very clever.
B: I think another reason why they are successful is . . .

9 LISTENING *Radio commercials*

A ▶ Listen to radio commercials for three different businesses.
What are two special features of each place?

	Maggie's	Sports Pro	Mexi-Grill
1.	....	....	....
2.	....	....	....

B ▶ Listen again. Complete each slogan.

1. "If you don't .... what you want in your .... , come .... ours!"
2. "We're here to .... you have .... !"
3. "You won't find a .... , ... meal – anywhere!"

10 INTERCHANGE 12 *Catchy slogans*

How well do you know the slogans companies use for their products?
Go to Interchange 12 on page 127.

11 DISCUSSION *TV commericials*

GROUP WORK Discuss these questions.

When you watch TV, do you pay attention to the commercials? Why or why not?
What commercials do you remember from the last time you watched TV?
What are some effective commercials you remember? What made them effective?
What is the funniest commercial you've ever seen? the dumbest? the most shocking?
Which celebrities have been in commercials? Has this affected your opinion of the product?
    Has it affected your opinion of the celebrity?
What differences are there between commercials today and commercials from the past?

12 WRITING *A commercial*

A Choose one of your favorite products. Read the questions and make notes
about the best way to sell it. Then write a one-minute radio or TV commercial.

What's good or unique about the product?
Why would someone want to buy or use it?
Can you think of a clever name or slogan?

B **GROUP WORK** Take turns presenting your
commercials. What is good about each one?
Can you give any suggestions to improve them?

> Are you looking for a high-quality
> TV that is also attractively designed?
> Buy a Star TV. Star is the most popular
> name in electronics because of its
> commitment to excellence and . . .

The Wrong Stuff

Look at the picture and the first sentence of the article. Why is market research important to companies that want to sell their products internationally?

If a business wants to sell its product internationally, it had better do some market research first. This is a lesson that some large American corporations have learned the hard way.

What's in a name?

Sometimes the problem is the name. When General Motors introduced its Chevy Nova into Latin America, it overlooked the fact that *No va* in Spanish means "It doesn't go." Sure enough, the Chevy Nova never went anywhere in Latin America.

Translation problems

Sometimes it's the slogan that doesn't work. No company knows this better than Pepsi-Cola, with its "Come alive with Pepsi!" campaign. The campaign was so successful in the United States that Pepsi translated its slogan literally for its international campaign. As it turned out, the translations weren't quite right. Pepsi was pleading with Germans to "Come out of the grave" and telling the Chinese that "Pepsi brings your ancestors back from the grave."

A picture's worth a thousand words

Other times, the problem involves packaging. A picture of a smiling, round-cheeked baby has helped sell countless jars of Gerber baby food. So when Gerber marketed its products in Africa, it kept the picture on the jar. What Gerber didn't realize was that in many African countries, the picture on the jar shows what the jar has in it.

Twist of fate

Even cultural factors can be involved. The cosmetics company Revlon made a costly mistake when they launched a new perfume in Brazil. The perfume smelled like Camellia flowers. It overlooked the fact that Camellia flowers are associated with funerals in Brazil. Unsurprisingly, the perfume failed. The entire Revlon brand suffered as many felt the company disrespected the culture.

Here's a great new car. The Nova!

It doesn't run?

A Read the article. Then for each statement, check (✓) True, False, or Not given.

	True	False	Not given
1. General Motors did a lot of research before naming the Chevy Nova.	☐	☐	☐
2. The "Come alive with Pepsi!" campaign worked well in the U.S.	☐	☐	☐
3. Pepsi still sold well in Germany and China.	☐	☐	☐
4. Gerber changed its packaging after the problem in Africa.	☐	☐	☐
5. The problem for Revlon was the name "Camellia."	☐	☐	☐
6. Revlon no longer sells cosmetics in Brazil.	☐	☐	☐

B Look at the marketing problems below. In each situation, was the problem related to the product's name (**N**) or slogan (**S**)?

.... 1. The Ford Fiera didn't sell well in Spain, where *fiera* means "ugly old woman."

.... 2. Braniff Airline's "Fly in leather" campaign was meant to promote its comfortable new seats. In Spanish, the company was telling passengers to "Fly with no clothes on."

C **GROUP WORK** Think of two products sold in your country: one that has sold well, and one that hasn't. Why did one sell well, but not the other? What changes could help the second product sell better?

Units 11–12 Progress check

SELF-ASSESSMENT

How well can you do these things? Check (✓) the boxes.

I can	Very well	OK	A little
Describe important life events and their consequences (Ex. 1)	☐	☐	☐
Describe and explain regrets about the past (Ex. 2)	☐	☐	☐
Describe hypothetical situations in the past (Ex. 2)	☐	☐	☐
Understand and give reasons for success (Ex. 3, 4)	☐	☐	☐
Describe the purpose of actions (Ex. 4)	☐	☐	☐

1 SPEAKING *Lessons to live by*

A What are two important events for each of these age groups? Complete the chart.

Children	Teenagers	People in their 20s	People in their 40s
....	....	....	....
....	....	....	....

B GROUP WORK Talk about the events. Why is each event important? What do people learn from each event?

A: Starting school is an important event for children.
B: Why is starting school an important milestone?
A: Once they start school, . . .

useful expressions	
after	once
as soon as	before
the moment	until
by the time	

2 GAME *A chain of events*

A Write three regrets you have about the past.

B GROUP WORK What if the situations were different? Take turns. One student expresses a regret. The next student adds a hypothetical result, and so on, for as long as you can.

A: I should have been more ambitious during college.
B: If you'd been more ambitious, you would have gone abroad.
C: If you'd gone abroad, you could have . . .

3 LISTENING *Success story*

A ▶ Listen to a business consultant discuss the factors necessary for a restaurant to be successful. Check (✓) the ones she says are important.

☐ advertising ☐ concept ☐ decor ☐ food ☐ location ☐ name

B ▶ Listen again. In your own words, write the reason why each factor is important.

Factor	Why is it important?
1.	....
2.	....
3.	....

4 DISCUSSION *The secrets of success*

A PAIR WORK Choose two businesses and discuss what they need to be successful. Then write three sentences describing the most important factors.

☐ a car wash ☐ a gourmet supermarket ☐ a juice bar
☐ a dance club ☐ a high-rise hotel ☐ a used clothing store

> 1. In order for a hotel to be successful, it has to be affordable.

B GROUP WORK Join another pair. Share your ideas. Do they agree?

A: We think in order for a hotel to be successful, it has to be affordable.
B: Really? But some of the most successful hotels are very expensive.

C GROUP WORK Now choose a popular business that you know about. What are the reasons for its success?

W Santiago

"I think W hotels are successful because the decor is so beautiful."

useful expressions	
It's successful because (of) . . .	It's become popular since . . .
It's popular due to . . .	It's famous for. . .
The reason it's successful is . . .	

WHAT'S NEXT?

Look at your Self-assessment again. Do you need to review anything?

 # That's a possibility.

1 SNAPSHOT

Pet Peeves

Why is it that some people...?

- are noisy eaters
- always ask for favors
- constantly interrupt
- are late all the time
- read over my shoulder on the subway
- chat online while talking on the phone
- always want to get in the last word
- throw their garbage in the recycling bin
- don't cover their mouths when they cough
- make popping sounds when they chew gum

Source: Interviews with people between the ages of 16 and 45

Which of the pet peeves do you have about people you know? Which one is the worst?
Underline a pet peeve you could be accused of. When and why are you guilty of it?
Are there any pet peeves in the list that don't annoy you?

2 CONVERSATION *What happened?*

A ▶ Listen and practice.

Jackie: You asked Beth to be here around 7:00, didn't you?
  Bill: Yes. What time is it now?
Jackie: It's almost 8:00. I wonder what happened.
  Bill: Hmm. She might have forgotten the time. Why don't I call and see if she's on her way?

A few minutes later

  Bill: I got her voice mail, so she must not have turned on her cell phone.
Jackie: I hope she didn't have a problem on the road. Her car could have broken down or something.
  Bill: Of course she may have simply forgotten and done something else today.
Jackie: No, she couldn't have forgotten – I just talked to her about it yesterday. I guess we should start without her.

B ▶ Listen to the rest of the conversation. What happened?

3 PRONUNCIATION *Reduction in past modals*

A Listen and practice. Notice how **have** is reduced in these sentences.

He must ~~have~~ forgotten the date.   She might ~~have~~ had a problem on the road.

B ▶ Listen and practice. Notice that **not** is not contracted or reduced in these sentences.

He may **not** have remembered it.   She must **not** have caught her bus.

4 GRAMMAR FOCUS

> ### Past modals for degrees of certainty ▶
>
> **It's almost certain.**
> She **must have left** already.
> She **must not have turned on** her phone.
>
> **It's not possible.**
> She **couldn't have been** at home.
>
> **It's possible.**
> She **may/might have forgotten** the time.
> She **may/might not have remembered** the time.
> Her car **could have broken down**.

A Read each situation and choose the best explanation. Then practice with a partner.
(Pay attention to the reduced forms in past modals.)

Situation

1. Maura couldn't keep her eyes open. ....
2. Brian got a call and looked worried. ....
3. The teacher looks very happy today. ....
4. Jane is in a terrible mood today. ....
5. Jeff was fired from his job. ....
6. My cousin is broke again. ....

Explanation

a. He may have gotten a raise.
b. She must not have gotten enough sleep.
c. He might not have done his work on time.
d. She could have had a fight with her boyfriend.
e. She must have spent too much last month.
f. He couldn't have heard good news.

B **PAIR WORK** Suggest different explanations for each situation in part A.

5 LISTENING *Jumping to conclusions*

A **GROUP WORK** What do you think happened? Offer an explanation for each event.

B ▶ Listen to the explanations for the two events in part A and take notes.
What *did* happen? How similar were your explanations?

6 SPEAKING What's your explanation?

A PAIR WORK What do you think were the reasons for these events? Suggest two different explanations for each.

1. Two people were having dinner in a restaurant. One suddenly got up and ran out of the restaurant.
2. A woman living alone returned home and found the TV and radio turned on. They weren't on when she went out.
3. Two friends met again after not seeing each other for many years. One looked at the other and burst out laughing.

B GROUP WORK Each student thinks of two situations like the ones in part A. Others suggest explanations.

A: Last night, a wife handed her husband a large bag of money.
B: Well, she might have returned some money she'd taken from him.

7 INTERCHANGE 13 Photo plays

What's your best explanation for some unusual events? Go to Interchange 13 on page 128.

8 PERSPECTIVES She's driving me crazy!

A   Listen to three friends talking to one another on the phone. Check (✓) the response you think is best for each person's problem.

Michi: Hi Molly. Ramona's mad because she thinks I didn't ask her to go hiking with us. I sent her four emails, but she never responded!

Michi   **Molly**

☐ Well, you know Ramona never answers emails. You should have called her on the phone.

☐ Oh, forget it! I wouldn't have sent so many messages. If Ramona can't bother to check her email, she'll just miss out on things.

Molly: Ramona, hi! I just got off the phone with Michi. She asked me for advice, but she never stops talking long enough to listen!

Molly   **Ramona**

☐ You could have been more understanding. Michi must have been upset and just needed to talk.

☐ I would have asked Michi to be quiet for a minute. How can you give her advice if she doesn't give you a chance to talk?

Ramona: Michi, I can't believe that Molly still has my notes! I needed them for a test today. She never returns things!

Ramona   **Michi**

☐ Molly shouldn't have kept your notes this long! But I wouldn't have lent them to her the week before a test.

☐ Oh, Molly may have just forgotten about them. I would have just borrowed someone else's notes.

B Do you talk about pet peeves with your friends? Do they give you advice?

9 GRAMMAR FOCUS

Past modals for judgments and suggestions

Judging past actions
You **should have called** her on the phone.
She **shouldn't have kept** your notes this long.

Suggesting alternative past actions
You **could have been** more understanding.
I **wouldn't have lent** them to her.

A Complete the conversations using past modals with the verbs given. Then practice with a partner.

1. A: I invited my boyfriend over to meet my parents, but he arrived wearing torn jeans. He looked so messy!
   B: Well, he .... (dress) neatly.
   I .... (ask) him to wear something nicer.

2. A: John borrowed my car and dented it. When he returned it, he didn't even say anything about it!
   B: He .... (tell) you! Well, I
   .... (not lend) it to him in the first place.
   He's a terrible driver.

3. A: I'm exhausted. Mary came over and stayed until 2:00 A.M.!
   B: She .... (not stay) so late. You
   .... (start) yawning. Maybe she would have gotten the hint!

4. A: Tom invited me to a play, but I ended up paying for us both!
   B: I .... (not pay) for him. He
   .... (not invite) you if he didn't have enough money.

B **PAIR WORK** Think of another suggestion or comment for each situation above.

10 WORD POWER *Reactions*

A Megan's boyfriend forgot her birthday. How does she react?
Match each reaction with the best example.

Reaction
1. an assumption ....
2. a criticism ....
3. a demand ....
4. an excuse ....
5. a prediction ....
6. a suggestion ....
7. a suspicion ....
8. a warning ....

Example
a. "If you do it again, you'll have to find a new girlfriend."
b. "I bet you were out with another woman!"
c. "You can be so inconsiderate."
d. "You'll probably forget our anniversary, too!"
e. "Now you have to take me out to dinner . . . twice."
f. "You must have wanted to break up with me."
g. "You know, you ought to buy me flowers."
h. "I know you've been busy lately. It just slipped your mind."

B **GROUP WORK** Imagine that someone was late for class, or choose another situation. Give an example of each reaction in the list above.

11 LISTENING *What should they have done?*

A ▶ Listen to descriptions of three situations. What would have been the best thing to do in each situation? Check (✓) the best suggestion.

1. ☐ Dennis should have called a locksmith.
   ☐ He should have broken a window.
   ☐ He did the right thing.

2. ☐ Diana should have turned up her radio to keep out the noise.
   ☐ She should have called the neighbors to see what was happening.
   ☐ She did the right thing.

3. ☐ Simon should have kept the ring for himself.
   ☐ He should have taken the ring and called the police.
   ☐ He did the right thing.

B PAIR WORK What would you have done in each situation in part A?

12 DISCUSSION *You could have . . .*

GROUP WORK Read each situation. Say what you could have or should have done.

"I went to my neighbor's house for dinner last night. He had cooked all day, but the food was awful! I didn't want to hurt his feelings, so I ate it."

"My friend forgot to do her homework, so she asked if she could look at mine. I did mine, but I told her I hadn't."

"I didn't have any money to buy my cousin a birthday present, so I gave her something I had received previously as a gift. My brother told my cousin and now she's mad at me."

"My friend started dating this guy I don't really like. She asked what I thought of him, and I told her the truth."

A: You should have told him you weren't feeling well.
B: Or you could have eaten it really slowly.
C: I think I would have . . .

13 WRITING *A complicated situation*

A Think of a complicated situation from your own experience. Write a paragraph describing the situation, but don't explain how you resolved it.

> One friend of mine is very demanding of my time. He wants to do everything with me, and I have a hard time saying no. I have other friends I want to spend time with as well. Last night, he asked me to spend all day Saturday with him. I didn't want to hurt his feelings. . . .

B PAIR WORK Exchange papers. Write a short paragraph about how you would have resolved your partner's situation.

C PAIR WORK Read your partner's resolution to your situation. Tell your partner how you resolved it. Whose resolution was better?

The Blue Lights of Silver Cliff

Look at the picture. What do you think the "blue lights" are?

Today, the town of Silver Cliff, Colorado, has a population of only 100 people. Once, however, it was a prosperous mining town where thousands came with dreams of finding silver and making their fortune.

Late one night in 1880, a group of miners were headed back to their camp after a good time in town. They were still laughing and joking as they approached the graveyard on a hill outside Silver Cliff. Then one of the men yelled and pointed toward the graveyard. The others fell silent. On top of each grave, they saw flamelike blue lights. These eerie lights seemed to be dancing on the graves, disappearing and then appearing again.

This was the first sighting of the blue lights of Silver Cliff. There have been many other sightings over the years. In 1969, Edward Lineham from National Geographic magazine visited the graveyard. Lineham's article tells of his experience: "I saw them. . . . Dim, round spots of blue-white light glowed ethereally among the graves. I . . . stepped forward for a better look. They vanished. I aimed my flashlight at one eerie glow and switched it on. It revealed only a tombstone."

Lineham and others have suggested various explanations for the lights. The lights might have been reflections of lights from the town, but Silver Cliff's lights seemed too dim to have this effect. They could have been caused by radioactive ore, though there's no evidence of radioactivity. They may also have been caused by gases from rotting matter. This usually happens in swamps, however, and the area around Silver Cliff is dry. Or, perhaps, the lights are from the helmets of dead miners wandering the hills in search of their fortune.

A Read the article. Then answer these questions.

1. How has Silver Cliff changed over the years?
2. Where were the blue lights first seen?
3. Who saw the blue lights first?
4. What do the blue lights look like?

B Which of these statements are facts? Which are opinions? Check (✓) Fact or Opinion.

	Fact	Opinion
1. Today, the town of Silver Cliff has a population of 100 people.	☐	☐
2. The miners saw flamelike blue lights on top of each grave.	☐	☐
3. Edward Lineham suggested various explanations for the lights.	☐	☐
4. The lights were actually reflections of lights from the town.	☐	☐
5. There was no evidence of radioactivity.	☐	☐
6. The lights were from the helmets of dead miners.	☐	☐

C **GROUP WORK** Which of the explanations for the blue lights do you think is the most satisfactory? Why? Can you think of any other possible explanations?

14 Behind the scenes

1 **SNAPSHOT**

Movie Firsts

The first...

- Movie-length music video – *Pink Floyd: The Wall* (1982)
- Advanced computer technology – *Terminator 2* (1991)
- Movie with Dolby Digital sound – *Batman Returns* (1992)
- Computer-animated feature film – *Toy Story* (1995)

- Movie to be released on DVD – *Twister* (1996)
- Movie to gross over $1 billion – *Titanic* (1998)
- 3-D movie to gross over $2 billion worldwide – *Avatar* (2009)
- Movie to make over $92 million in one day – *Harry Potter and the Deathly Hallows – Part 2* (2011)

Sources: www.imdb.com; www.listology.com

Have you seen any of these movies? Did you enjoy them?
What's the most popular movie playing right now? Have you seen it? Do you plan to?
Are there many movies made in your country? Name a few of your favorites.

2 CONVERSATION *Movies are hard work!*

A ▶ Listen and practice.

Ryan: Working on movies must be really exciting.
Nina: Oh, yeah, but it's also very hard work.
A one-minute scene in a film can take days to shoot.
Ryan: Really? Why is that?
Nina: Well, a scene isn't filmed just once. Lots of different shots have to be taken. Only the best ones are used in the final film.
Ryan: So, how many times does a typical scene need to be shot?
Nina: It depends, but sometimes as many as 20 times. One scene may be shot from five or six different angles.
Ryan: Wow! I didn't realize that.
Nina: Why don't you come visit the studio? I can show you how things are done.
Ryan: Great, I'd love to!

B ▶ Listen to the rest of the conversation. What else makes working on movies difficult?

3 GRAMMAR FOCUS

The passive to describe process ▶

is/are + past participle
A scene **isn't filmed** just once.
Only the best shots **are used**.

Modal + be + past participle
One scene **may be shot** from five or six different angles.
Lots of different shots **have to be taken**.

A The sentences below describe how a movie is made. First, complete the sentences using the passive. Then compare with a partner.

Before filming

☐ To complete the script, it has to .... (divide) into scenes, and the filming details need to .... (write out).

1 First, an outline of the script has to .... (prepare).

☐ Next, actors .... (choose), locations .... (pick), and costumes .... (design). Filming can then begin.

☐ Then the outline .... (expand) into a script.

☐ After the script .... (complete), a director must .... (hire).

During and after filming

☐ The final film you see on the screen .... (create) by the director and editor out of thousands of different shots.

☐ Soon after the film has been edited, music .... (compose) and sound effects may .... (add).

☐ After the filming .... (finish), the different shots can then .... (put together) by the editor and director.

6 Once shooting begins, different shots .... (film) separately. Scenes may .... (not shoot) in sequence.

B **PAIR WORK** Number the sentences in part A (before filming: from 1 to 5; during and after filming: from 6 to 9).

4 LISTENING *I love my job!*

A ▶ Listen to an interview with a TV producer. Write down three things a producer does.

Things a producer does	Personality traits
1.	....
2.	....
3.	....

B ▶ Listen again. What are three personality traits a producer should have? Complete the chart.

5 SPEAKING *Step by step*

A PAIR WORK What do you think is required to prepare for a theater performance?
Put the pictures in order and describe the steps. Use the vocabulary to help you.

make the costumes

rehearse the lines

build the sets

choose the actors

find a venue

write the script

A: Preparing for a theater performance requires many steps.
     First, the script must be written.
B: Right! And after that, the actors are chosen.
A: I agree. Then . . .

B PAIR WORK Choose one of these topics. Come up with as many steps as you can.

creating a student newspaper   planning a wedding   preparing for a rock concert
making a short video   preparing for a fashion show putting on a school musical

C GROUP WORK Share your information from part B with another pair.

6 WRITING *Describing a process*

A Write about one of the topics from Exercise 5 or use your own idea.
Describe the different steps in the process.

> Putting on a school musical requires a lot of planning.
> First, the director and production team must be chosen.
> Then the dates for the musical should be decided.
> After that, the actual musical can be chosen. Then
> auditions for the various roles can be held and . . .

B PAIR WORK Read your partner's paper. Can you think of
any more steps?

7 WORD POWER *Media professions*

A What kind of jobs are these? Complete the chart with the compound nouns.

computer programmer   network installer   photo editor   software designer
editorial director   newscaster   movie extra   stunt person
film composer   page designer   sitcom writer   talk show host

Film jobs	Publishing jobs	TV jobs	Computer jobs
....	....	....	....
....	....	....	....
....	....	....	....

B GROUP WORK Choose four jobs from part A and describe what they do.

"A computer programmer writes the instructions that direct computers to process information."

8 PERSPECTIVES *Quiz show*

A ▶ Listen to a quiz show. Can you guess the occupations?

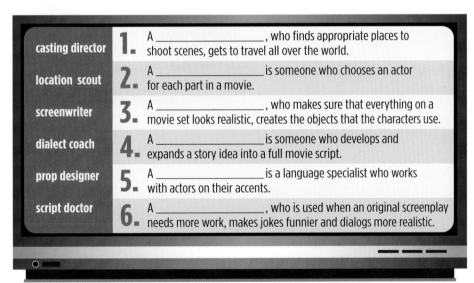

casting director

location scout

screenwriter

dialect coach

prop designer

script doctor

1. A _____, who finds appropriate places to shoot scenes, gets to travel all over the world.

2. A _____ is someone who chooses an actor for each part in a movie.

3. A _____, who makes sure that everything on a movie set looks realistic, creates the objects that the characters use.

4. A _____ is someone who develops and expands a story idea into a full movie script.

5. A _____ is a language specialist who works with actors on their accents.

6. A _____, who is used when an original screenplay needs more work, makes jokes funnier and dialogs more realistic.

B Which of the jobs in part A do you think would be the most interesting? Why? Tell the class.

9 PRONUNCIATION *Review of stress in compound nouns*

A ▶ Listen and practice. Notice how the first word in a compound noun usually receives greater stress.

newscaster   photo editor   movie extra   sitcom writer   stunt person

B Practice the sentences in Exercise 8. Pay attention to the word stress in the compound nouns.

Defining and non-defining relative clauses ▶

Defining relative clauses are used to identify people.

A dialect coach is a language specialist. ⟶ A dialect coach is a language specialist **who/that**
She works with actors on their accents. **works with actors on their accents**.

Non-defining relative clauses give further information about people.

A location scout finds places to shoot ⟶ A location scout, **who finds places to**
scenes. He travels all over the world. **shoot scenes**, travels all over the world.

A Do these sentences contain defining (**D**) or non-defining (**ND**) clauses? Add commas to the non-defining clauses. Then compare with a partner.

a stunt person

1. A stunt person is someone who "stands in" for an actor during dangerous scenes. ....
2. A computer-graphics supervisor who needs advanced technical knowledge often spends millions of dollars on computer graphics. ....
3. A stagehand is the person who moves the sets on stage in a theater production. ....
4. A movie producer who controls the budget decides how money will be spent. ....

B Add the non-defining relative clauses in parentheses to the sentences.

1. A movie extra appears in the background scenes.
   (who never has any lines)
   ....
   ....

2. A newscaster presents the news and introduces videos from reporters.
   (who should be trustworthy)
   ....
   ....

3. A photo editor selects the photos that go into magazines.
   (who is responsible for the quality and content of images)
   ....
   ....

4. A film composer must know music theory and interpretation.
   (who writes the background music for movies)
   ....
   ....

C Write three sentences with relative clauses about jobs you know. Compare with a partner.

11 *INTERCHANGE 14* *Who makes it happen?*

What kinds of people does it take to make a movie? Go to Interchange 14 on page 129.

Hooray for Bollywood!

Scan the article. Who do you think it was written for?
☐ people in the film industry ☐ the general public ☐ fans of Bollywood movies

1 A storm forces a plane to make an emergency landing on a deserted island. The only shelter is a spooky house, where a murderer begins killing passengers. So what do these defenseless people do? They have a beach party and perform an elaborate song-and-dance number.

2 This is the world of Bollywood. The scene described above is from the classic Indian film *Gumnaam*, which was made in the 1960s. It is typical of the kind of movies that are still made in India today.

3 For as long as Hollywood has existed, there has also been an Indian film industry. Because it is based in Mumbai (formerly Bombay), it is popularly called Bollywood – from the words Bombay and Hollywood. While it is as old as Hollywood, it is much bigger. Bollywood currently has the largest movie industry in the world. It produces more than 1,100 films a year – and as many as 20 million people a day pack into movie theaters to see Bollywood films.

4 While there are many types of films made in India, the most popular are the movies made in Bollywood. The films, which are made in the Hindi language, generally deal with Indian history and social issues. The average Bollywood film runs about three hours but audiences don't seem to mind the length. The stories are melodramatic: Heroes drive around in flashy cars, actresses twirl around in beautiful costumes, and the poor boy always triumphs against the rich villain. They also feature many musical numbers, usually love songs.

5 Although the films may seem exaggerated to some, that's not how most filmgoers feel. These movies and their stars are beloved by audiences throughout Asia, Africa, and the Middle East. "Every South Asian grows up with some kind of connection to Bollywood," notes Indian writer Suketu Mehta. "In certain ways, it's what unites us."

A Read the article. Find and underline a sentence in the article that answers each question below.

1. How does Bollywood compare to Hollywood?
2. How many Bollywood films are made every year?
3. How long is a typical Bollywood movie?
4. How do audiences feel about the stars of Bollywood movies?

B Find these sentences in the article. Decide whether each sentence is the main idea or a supporting idea in that paragraph. Check (✓) the correct boxes.

	Main idea	Supporting idea
1. This is the world of Bollywood. (par. 2)	☐	☐
2. It produces more than . . . to see Bollywood films. (par. 3)	☐	☐
3. While there are many . . . made in Bollywood. (par. 4)	☐	☐
4. The average Bollywood film . . . mind the length. (par. 4)	☐	☐
5. Although the films may seem . . . filmgoers feel. (par. 5)	☐	☐

C **GROUP WORK** Have you ever seen a Bollywood movie? If so, how did you like it?

Units 13–14 Progress check

SELF-ASSESSMENT

How well can you do these things? Check (✓) the boxes.

I can	Very well	OK	A little
Understand and speculate about past events (Ex. 1)	☐	☐	☐
Make judgments and suggestions about past events (Ex. 2)	☐	☐	☐
Describe processes (Ex. 3)	☐	☐	☐
Describe people's appearance, personality, and typical behavior (Ex. 4)	☐	☐	☐

1 LISTENING *Where did it take place?*

A ▶ Listen to three conversations. Where do you think each conversation takes place? What do you think might have happened? Take notes.

Where the conversation takes place	What might have happened
1.	....
2.	....
3.	....

B **PAIR WORK** Compare your notes. Decide on what happened.

2 DISCUSSION *Tricky situations*

A **PAIR WORK** React to these situations. First, make a judgment or suggestion using a past modal. Then add another statement using the reaction in parentheses.

1. John was driving too fast, and the police stopped him. (a warning)
2. Lisa got an F on her English test. (a criticism)
3. Bill went shopping and spent too much money. (an excuse)
4. Crystal is late to class every morning. (a suggestion)
5. Oscar studied all night for his final exam and didn't sleep at all. (a prediction)

"John shouldn't have driven so fast. He'd better be careful, or . . ."

B **GROUP WORK** Join another pair and compare your comments. Who has the most interesting reaction to each situation?

3 GAME *From first to last*

A GROUP WORK Look at these topics. Set a time limit. Talk with your group and write as many steps as you can between the first and last parts of each process.

sending an email

making a cup of tea

First, the computer has to be turned on.

....

....

....

....

....

Finally, the email is delivered to the person's in-box.

First, some water must be boiled.

....

....

....

....

....

Finally, the tea has to be poured from the teapot into the cup.

B CLASS ACTIVITY Compare your answers. Which group has the most steps?

4 SPEAKING *People in your life*

A Complete these statements about people in your life.

My mother is a person who ....
My neighbor, who .... , always ....
My father is a .... who ....
My teacher, who .... , is ....
My best friend is someone that ....

B PAIR WORK Compare your answers. Ask two follow-up questions about each of your partner's statements.

A: My mother is a person who takes care of everyone's needs before her own.
B: Does she ever get tired of helping everyone but herself?

WHAT'S NEXT?

Look at your Self-assessment again. Do you need to review anything?

 # There should be a law!

It's Against the Law!

In the United States and Canada	In other countries

Police

In the United States and Canada
- In Arizona, you may go to prison for 25 years if you cut down a saguaro cactus.
- In New Britain, Connecticut, fire trucks must travel at 25 miles per hour even when going to a fire.
- In the state of Washington, it is illegal to pretend your parents are rich.
- In Canada, 35% of radio broadcasting time must have Canadian content.

In other countries
- In Switzerland, it's an offense to hang clothes out to dry on a Sunday.
- In Australia, it is illegal to walk on the right side of footpaths.
- It is against the law not to flush a public toilet in Singapore.
- In Finland, taxi drivers must pay royalties if they play music for customers.

Sources: www.dumblaws.com

Which of these laws would you like to have in your city or country? Why?
Can you think of reasons for these laws?
Do you know of any other unusual laws?

2 *PERSPECTIVES*

A ▶ Listen to people make recommendations at a community meeting. Would you agree with these proposals if they were made in your community? Check (✓) your opinion.

Community Meeting Notes

	strongly agree	somewhat agree	disagree
1. Cyclists should be required to wear helmets.	☐	☐	☐
2. Pet owners shouldn't be allowed to walk dogs without a leash.	☐	☐	☐
3. People ought to be required to end parties at midnight.	☐	☐	☐
4. Something has got to be done to stop littering.	☐	☐	☐
5. People mustn't be permitted to park motorcycles on the sidewalks.	☐	☐	☐
6. Laws must be passed to control the noise from car alarms.	☐	☐	☐
7. Drivers should only be permitted to honk their horns in case of an emergency.	☐	☐	☐

B **GROUP WORK** Compare your opinions. If you have different opinions, give reasons for your opinions to try to get your classmates to agree with you.

3 GRAMMAR FOCUS

Giving recommendations and opinions ⊙

When you think something is a good idea
Cyclists **should be required** to wear a helmet.
Pet owners **shouldn't be allowed** to walk dogs without a leash.
People **ought (not) to be required** to end parties at midnight.

When you think something is absolutely necessary
Laws **must be passed** to control the noise from car alarms.
People **mustn't be permitted** to park motorcycles on the sidewalks.
A rule **has to be made** to require cycling lanes on city streets.
Something **has got to be done** to stop littering.

A Complete the sentences positively or negatively. Choose a modal that shows how strongly you feel about these issues.

1. People .... (allow) to use cell phones while driving.
2. Young people .... (permit) to get married before age 15.
3. Companies .... (require) to give workers periodic breaks.
4. People .... (allow) to have pets in high-rise apartments.
5. Scientists .... (permit) to use animals for research.
6. Laws .... (pass) to ban the sale of handguns.
7. The sale of fur products .... (prohibit).
8. Something .... (do) to stop clubs from staying open so late.

B GROUP WORK Compare your statements. Do you agree with one another? If not, why not?

A: People shouldn't be allowed to use cell phones while driving. It's dangerous.
B: You may have a point, but laws shouldn't be passed to prevent it. That's too strict.
C: Maybe, but in my opinion, . . .

4 DISCUSSION What's your opinion?

A GROUP WORK Think of three reasons for, and three reasons against, each idea below. Then discuss your views. As a group, form an opinion about each idea.

imposing strict dress codes for students
requiring people to do volunteer work
paying teachers less when their students fail

offering a different opinion
That sounds interesting, but I think . . .
That's not a bad idea. On the other hand, I feel . . .
You may have a point. However, I think . . .

A: What do you think about imposing strict dress codes for students?
B: I think it's a terrible idea! Students shouldn't be required . . .

B CLASS ACTIVITY Share your group's opinions and reasons. Who has the most persuasive reasons for and against each position?

There should be a law! ▪ 101

5 LISTENING *What should be done?*

A ⏵ Listen to people discuss problems. What solutions do they suggest? Take notes in the chart.

1. people talking loudly on cell phones in restaurants

2. car alarms going off at night

3. telemarketing salespeople calling too often

Solutions
1. ....
2. ....
3. ....

B GROUP WORK Do you agree or disagree with the solutions? What do you think should be done about each problem?

6 INTERCHANGE 15 *You be the judge!*

What if you could make the rules? Go to Interchange 15 on page 130.

7 WORD POWER *Local concerns*

A PAIR WORK Which of these issues are problems in your community? Check (✓) the appropriate boxes.

- ☐ bullying
- ☐ company outsourcing
- ☐ graffiti
- ☐ homelessness
- ☐ inadequate health care
- ☐ lack of affordable child care
- ☐ noise pollution
- ☐ overcrowded classrooms
- ☐ stray animals
- ☐ street crime

noise pollution

B GROUP WORK Join another pair of students. Which three problems concern your group the most? What should or can be done about them?

8 CONVERSATION *It isn't cheap, is it?*

A ▶ Listen and practice.

Sarah: Health insurance, child-care bills, rent! Now that I'm going to school and only working part-time, I have a hard time making ends meet.

Todd: Health insurance is really expensive, isn't it?

Sarah: Yeah! My company used to pay for it when I was working full-time.

Todd: And child care isn't cheap, is it?

Sarah: No, it's not. After I pay for rent and groceries, almost all my money goes to pay for my son's day care.

Todd: Colleges should provide free day care for students with children.

Sarah: I think so, too. But they don't have any services like that at my school.

B ▶ Listen to the rest of the conversation. What is Todd concerned about?

9 GRAMMAR FOCUS

> ### Tag questions for opinions ▶
>
> | **Affirmative statement + negative tag** | **Negative statement + affirmative tag** |
> |---|---|
> | Health insurance is really expensive, **isn't it**? | Child care isn't cheap, **is it**? |
> | There are lots of criminals in the city, **aren't there**? | There aren't enough police, **are there**? |
> | Graffiti makes everything look ugly, **doesn't it**? | People don't care about our city, **do they**? |
> | Colleges should provide day care, **shouldn't they**? | You can't find affordable child care, **can you**? |

A Add tag questions to these statements. Then compare with a partner.

1. You can't escape advertising nowadays, . . . ?
2. There aren't any noise pollution laws, . . . ?
3. School bullying is a major problem here, . . . ?
4. Overcrowded classrooms can be hard to manage, . . . ?
5. The sales tax should be lowered, . . . ?
6. It isn't easy to save money these days, . . . ?
7. The city doesn't do enough for stray animals, . . . ?
8. There are more homeless people on the streets, . . . ?

B What are some things you feel strongly about in your school or city? Write six statements with tag questions.

C **GROUP WORK** Take turns reading your statements. Other students respond by giving their opinions.

A: The food in the cafeteria is terrible, isn't it?
B: Yes, it is. They should get a new cook.
C: On the other hand, I like the hamburgers because . . .

10 PRONUNCIATION *Intonation in tag questions*

A ◉ Listen and practice. Use falling intonation in tag questions when you are giving an opinion and expect the other person to agree.

Street crime is a terrible problem, isn't it?

People should have access to quality health care, shouldn't they?

B **PAIR WORK** Take turns reading the statements with tag questions from Exercise 9, part A. Give your own opinions when responding.

11 LISTENING *You agree, don't you?*

A ◉ Listen to people give their opinions about current issues in the news. What issues are they talking about?

Issue	Opinions for	Opinions against
1.	....	....
	....	....
2.	....	....
	....	....

B ◉ Listen again. What opinions do you hear? Complete the chart.

C **GROUP WORK** What do you think about the issues in part A?

12 WRITING *A new law*

A Think about a local problem that needs to be solved, and write a persuasive essay suggesting a new law to help solve it. Be creative! Use these questions to help you.

What is the problem, and how does it affect your community?
What can be done to help solve it?
Who might disagree with you, and how will you convince them
    that your law is a good idea?

> I think students in our town should be required to wear school uniforms. Students shouldn't be permitted to wear the latest fashions because this promotes jealousy and competition. Also, students would be able to concentrate on their studies better if . . .

B **GROUP WORK** Try to convince your classmates to pass your new law. Then vote on it.

How Serious Is Plagiarism?

Read the title and first paragraph of the article. What do you think the word plagiarism means?

In 2002, a biology teacher in Kansas – a state in the American Midwest – made national, and even international, news. After Christine Pelton discovered that 28 of her 118 students had plagiarized parts of a major project, she gave them failing grades. Although this was the school policy, the students' parents complained. The school board directed Ms. Pelton to change the punishment: They told her that 600 points should be taken from the offenders, rather than the entire 1,800 points. Ms. Pelton resigned in protest.

Why did this become such a significant story? Perhaps it is because so many people feel strongly about what is right and wrong. The incident raised some important questions: What is plagiarism? How serious is it?

The simplest form of plagiarism occurs when someone copies material without giving credit to the source. However, there are also more serious forms, such as when a student pays someone else to write an essay.

Some people claim that copying is necessary to do well in school. They have realized that their own words are not as good as someone else's. Another common argument is that everyone does it, so it's not a big deal. In fact, it has been learned that even some highly respected figures, including Martin Luther King Jr., have plagiarized.

Although some people find reasons to justify plagiarism, others feel the issue is clear-cut: They feel it is morally wrong, and consider it stealing – a theft of ideas rather than money. These people believe that students who plagiarize benefit unfairly. They receive a better grade than they deserve.

So what about the incident in Kansas? Was the original punishment too severe? Do teachers have the right to tell students and parents what is right or wrong? Ms. Pelton would probably say that the job of a teacher is to do exactly that.

A Read the article. Then number these sentences from 1 (first event) to 6 (last event).

.... a. The teacher's story appeared in national news.
.... b. The teacher gave the students failing grades.
.... c. The students' parents were angry.
.... d. The teacher left her job.
.... e. The group of students cheated on an assignment.
.... f. The school board told the teacher to change the scores.

B Complete the chart with the arguments for and against plagiarism presented in the article.

Arguments to justify plagiarism	Arguments against plagiarism
1.	....
2.	....

C **GROUP WORK** Is it ever OK to copy other people's work? Why or why not?
Should teachers have the right to tell students and parents what is right or wrong?

16 Challenges and accomplishments

1 SNAPSHOT

VOLUNTEER! What are you interested in? Consider these volunteering opportunities.

COSTA RICA
▶ helping at a wildlife center
▶ monitoring endangered birds
▶ assisting with reforestation
▶ teaching computer skills
▶ organizing environmental activities

THAILAND
▶ repairing rural roads
▶ building schools
▶ designing websites
▶ taking care of elephants
▶ working in rural health clinics

MOZAMBIQUE
▶ building houses
▶ working at an orphanage
▶ conducting health surveys
▶ teaching English
▶ working on a marine conservation project

Sources: www.volunteerabroad.com; www.kayavolunteer.com

Which project sounds the most interesting? the least interesting?
Can you think of any other interesting projects that volunteers could do?
Do you know anyone who has volunteered? What did they do?

2 PERSPECTIVES *Volunteers talk about their work.*

A ⏵ Listen to people talk about their volunteer work. What kind of work do they do? Write the names in the sentences below.

> The most rewarding thing about helping them is learning from their years of experience.
> —Paul

> One of the most difficult aspects of working abroad is being away from my family.
> —Sho-fang

> One of the rewards of working with them is experiencing their youthful energy and playfulness.
> —Mariela

> The most challenging thing about doing this type of work is determining their strengths and weaknesses.
> —Jack

1. .... **teaches in a developing country.**
2. .... **tutors in an adult literacy program.**
3. .... **visits senior citizens in a nursing home.**
4. .... **plays games with children in an orphanage.**

B Which kind of volunteer work would you prefer to do? What do you think would be rewarding or challenging about it?

3 GRAMMAR FOCUS

> ### Complex noun phrases containing gerunds ▶
>
> **The most rewarding thing about helping them** is learning from their years of experience.
> **One of the most difficult aspects of working abroad** is being away from my family.
> **One of the rewards of working with them** is experiencing their youthful energy.

A PAIR WORK Match the questions and responses. Then ask and answer the questions. Respond using a complex noun phrase followed by a gerund.

Questions

1. What's the most challenging thing about working from home? ....
2. What's the best thing about being a police officer? ....
3. What's one of the rewards of being a teacher? ....
4. What's one of the most difficult things about being an emergency-room nurse? ....
5. What's one of the most interesting aspects of working abroad? ....
6. What's one of the most difficult aspects of doing volunteer work? ....
7. What's the hardest part about being overseas? ....

Responses

a. dealing with life-or-death situations every day
b. finding enough time to do it on a regular basis
c. learning how people in other cultures live and think
d. helping people learn things that they couldn't learn on their own
e. not talking with my family regularly
f. getting to know people from all parts of society
g. not being distracted by household chores or hobbies

A: What's the most challenging thing about working from home?
B: The most challenging thing about working from home is not being distracted by household chores or hobbies.

B GROUP WORK Ask the questions in part A again and answer with your own ideas.

4 PRONUNCIATION Stress and rhythm

A Listen and practice. Notice how stressed words and syllables occur with a regular rhythm.

   ●   ●   ●   ●

The most rewarding thing │ about traveling │ is learning │ about other cultures.

   ●   ●   ●   ●   ●

The most frustrating thing │ about working │ in a foreign country │ is missing │ friends and family.

B PAIR WORK Take turns reading the sentences in the grammar box in Exercise 3. Pay attention to stress and rhythm.

5 INTERCHANGE 16 *Viewpoints*

Take a survey about volunteering. Go to Interchange 16 on page 131.

6 LISTENING *Challenges and rewards*

▶ Listen to these people talk about their work. What is the biggest challenge of each person's job? What is the greatest reward? Complete the chart.

	Biggest challenge	Greatest reward
1. psychologist	....	....
2. camp counselor	....	....
3. firefighter	....	....

7 WORD POWER *Antonyms*

A Complete the pairs of opposites with the words in the box. Then compare with a partner.

compassionate	cynical	dependent	rigid	timid	unimaginative

1. adaptable   ≠ ....
2. courageous   ≠ ....
3. insensitive ≠ ....

4. resourceful   ≠ ....
5. self-sufficient ≠ ....
6. upbeat   ≠ ....

B GROUP WORK How many words or things can you associate with each word in part A?

A: What words or things do you associate with *adaptable*?
B: Flexible.
C: Easy to get along with.

8 DISCUSSION *Rewarding work*

GROUP WORK What are the special challenges and rewards of working in these situations? Would you ever consider working in one of these areas? Why or why not?

working with animals
teaching gifted children
cooking food at a homeless shelter
working for a nonprofit organization
working in a home for the visually impaired

A: I suppose the most challenging thing about working with animals is . . .
B: But one of the rewards of working with animals must be . . .

9 CONVERSATION *I've managed to get good grades, but...*

A ▶ Listen and practice.

Uncle Ed: Happy birthday, Alison! So how does it feel to be 21?

Alison: Kind of strange. I suddenly feel a little anxious, like I'm not moving ahead fast enough.

Uncle Ed: But don't you think you've accomplished quite a bit in the last few years?

Alison: Oh, I've managed to get good grades, but I still haven't been able to decide on a career.

Uncle Ed: Well, what do you hope you'll have achieved by the time you're 30?

Alison: For one thing, I hope I'll have seen more of the world. But more important than that, I'd like to have made a good start on my career by then.

B CLASS ACTIVITY How similar are you to Alison? Are you satisfied with your accomplishments so far? What do you want to accomplish next?

10 GRAMMAR FOCUS

> ### Accomplishments and goals ▶
>
> | **Accomplishments with the present perfect or simple past** | **Goals with the future perfect or would like to have + past participle** |
> |---|---|
> | I**'ve managed** to get good grades.
(I **managed** to . . .)
I**'ve been able** to accomplish a lot in college.
(I **was able** to . . .) | What do you hope you**'ll have achieved**?
I hope I**'ll have seen** more of the world.
I**'d like to have made** a good start on my career. |

A What are some of your accomplishments from the last five years? Check (✓) the statements that are true for you. Then think of four more statements about yourself.

☐ 1. I've met the person who's right for me.
☐ 2. I've learned some important life skills.
☐ 3. I was able to complete my degree.
☐ 4. I've made an important career move.

B What are some goals you would like to have accomplished in the future? Complete the sentences.

1. By this time next year, I hope I'll have . . .
2. Three years from now, I'd like to have . . .
3. In ten years, I'd like to have . . .
4. By the time I'm 60, I hope I'll have . . .

C GROUP WORK Compare your sentences in parts A and B. What accomplishments do you have in common? What goals?

11 *LISTENING* *Future plans*

A ▶ Listen to three young people discuss their plans for the future. What do they hope they'll have achieved by the time they are 30?

1. Rick	2. Jasmine	3. Bianca
....	....	....
....	....	....
....	....	....

B **PAIR WORK** Who do you think has the most realistic expectations?

12 *WRITING* *A personal statement for an application*

A Imagine you are applying to a school or for a job that requires a personal statement. Use these questions to organize your ideas. Make notes and then write a draft.

1. What has your greatest accomplishment been? Has it changed you in any way? How?
2. What are some interesting or unusual facts about yourself that make you a good choice for the job or school?
3. What is something you hope to have achieved ten years from now? When, why, and how will you reach this goal? Will achieving it change you? Why or why not?

> I think my greatest accomplishment has been finally getting my diploma at age 30. I've been able to achieve many things in school with the support of my family, and . . .
>
> There are two things I'd really like to have achieved by the time I'm 40. First, I hope I'll have done some traveling. . . .

B **GROUP WORK** Share your statements and discuss each person's accomplishments and goals. Who has the most unusual accomplishment or goal? the most realistic? the most ambitious?

13 *READING*

Young and Gifted

Scan the article. Who is happy to spend lots of time alone?
Who is multilingual? Who has done community service?

Ali Pirhani comes from Hamedan in Iran. By the age of five, he could speak French, German, and English as well as his native language, Farsi. By the age of 24, he was a fluent speaker of 19 languages, including such diverse languages as Hindi, Arabic, Turkish, and Swahili. Ali says, "I have always been interested in communicating with people from different nations in order to learn from them. I think learning languages is one of the best ways to learn about their cultures." He has established a polyglot center to promote multilingualism by conducting research into language learning.

A lot of people have sailed, nonstop and alone, around the world, but Jessica Watson claims to be the first 16-year-old to have done so. On May 15, 2010, she returned to Sydney, Australia, after 210 days at sea. However, her claim is not recognized by the World Sailing Speed Record Council. As its name suggests, the council only considers speed records, not factors such as age. Also, the council's minimum distance to qualify for circumnavigation is 26,000 nautical miles, but Jessica's route, via the southern oceans, was shorter than this. Her reaction to the council's decision? "It really doesn't bother me."

At age 10, Samson Diamond joined a music project in Soweto, South Africa, and picked up a violin. He soon became leader of the project's Buskaid Soweto String Ensemble, which plays classical music. Later, he obtained a master's degree in music performance. He has also used his talent to serve poor communities in England, Jamaica, and his home country by teaching underprivileged people how to empower themselves through music. He says, "My philosophy is 'the further you go, the further there is to go. Never stop searching.'"

A Read the article. Find the words in *italics* in the article.
Then match each word with its meaning.

.... 1. *diverse*
.... 2. *polyglot*
.... 3. *circumnavigation*
.... 4. *underprivileged*

a. sailing (or flying) around something
b. poor, not having the things most people have
c. different
d. speaking or using many different languages

B Which statements are inferences (**I**)? Which are restatements (**R**)?
Which are not given (**NG**)?

.... 1. Ali Pirhani learned a lot of languages when he was a teenager.
.... 2. He believes that culture and language are closely connected.
.... 3. Jessica Watson circumnavigated the world via the southern oceans.
.... 4. She plans to circumnavigate the world via a longer route.
.... 5. Samson Diamond was a fast learner on the violin
.... 6. He wants young people to play sports as well as music.

C GROUP WORK Which person do you think is making the biggest contribution to society? Why?
What personal characteristics made it possible for him or her to achieve so much?

Units 15–16 Progress check

SELF-ASSESSMENT

How well can you do these things? Check (✓) the boxes.

I can	Very well	OK	A little
Give recommendations and opinions about rules (Ex. 1)	☐	☐	☐
Understand and express opinions, and seek agreement (Ex. 2)	☐	☐	☐
Describe qualities necessary to achieve particular goals (Ex. 3)	☐	☐	☐
Describe challenges connected with particular goals (Ex. 3)	☐	☐	☐
Ask about and describe personal achievements and ambitions (Ex. 4)	☐	☐	☐

1 DISCUSSION *Setting the rules*

A PAIR WORK What kinds of rules do you think should be made for these places? Talk with your partner and make three rules for each. (Have fun! Don't make your rules too serious.)

a health club   an apartment building
a school   the school library

B GROUP WORK Join another pair. Share your ideas. Do they agree?

A: People should be required to use every machine in a health club.
B: That sounds interesting. Why?
A: Well, for one thing, people would be in better shape!

2 LISTENING *Social issues*

A ▶ Listen to people give opinions. Check (✓) the correct responses.

1. ☐ Yes, it is.
   ☐ Yes, they are.

2. ☐ Yes, they do.
   ☐ Yes, they should.

3. ☐ Yes, we do.
   ☐ Yes, it does.

4. ☐ Yes, it does.
   ☐ Yes, it should.

5. ☐ No, they can't.
   ☐ No, it isn't.

6. ☐ No, they don't.
   ☐ No, you can't.

B PAIR WORK Write a tag question for each response you did not check.

1. Stray animals are so sad, aren't they? Yes, they are.

3 DISCUSSION *What does it take?*

A GROUP WORK What qualities are good or bad if you want to accomplish these goals? Talk with the group and decide on two qualities for each.

Goals	Qualities		
hike across your country conduct an orchestra make a low-budget movie become a salsa instructor	adaptable compassionate courageous cynical	dependent insensitive resourceful rigid	self-sufficient timid unimaginative upbeat

A: To hike across your country, you need to be courageous.
B: Yeah, and you can't be dependent on anyone.

B GROUP WORK What do you think would be the most challenging things about achieving the goals in part A? How would you overcome the challenges?

A: I think the most challenging thing about hiking across your country would be feeling lonely all the time.
B: I agree. So how would you cope with loneliness?

4 ROLE PLAY *Interview*

Student A: Student B is going to interview you for the school website. Think about your accomplishments and goals. Then answer the questions.

Student B: Imagine you are interviewing Student A for the school website. Add two questions to the notebook. Then start the interview.

Change roles and try the role play again.

What have you managed to accomplish in school? What would you like to have achieved by the time you graduate?

Are you happy with your home? Do you hope you will move someday? Where would you like to live?

Have you been able to accomplish a lot in your career? Where do you hope you'll be in five years?

_____

_____

WHAT'S NEXT?

Look at your Self-assessment again. Do you need to review anything?

Interchange activities

A PAIR WORK What is your personality type? Take turns using this quiz to interview each other. Then calculate your answers and find out which category best describes you.

PERSONALITY QUIZ

1. When you work on a big project, do you:
   a. try to finish it as quickly as possible?
   b. work at it over a long period of time?
   c. put it off as long as possible?

2. When you do an assignment, do you:
   a. try to do a first-class job so people will notice?
   b. do it as well as you can without worrying too much about it?
   c. do only what you must to get it done?

3. When faced with a difficult challenge, do you:
   a. look forward to facing it?
   b. worry about dealing with it?
   c. try to avoid it?

4. Do you think the best way to get the most out of a day is to:
   a. do as many things as possible?
   b. take your time to get things done?
   c. do only those things you really have to?

5. When you need to do a big task, do you:
   a. do it yourself?
   b. work with others to get it done?
   c. not do it?

6. When something doesn't work out the way you want it to, do you:
   a. get angry with yourself and others?
   b. think calmly about what to do next?
   c. give up, because it wasn't important anyway?

7. When people take a long time to finish something, do you:
   a. get impatient and do it yourself?
   b. gently ask them to do it more quickly?
   c. let them take their time?

8. If you compare your goals with your friends' goals, do you:
   a. want to accomplish greater things than they do?
   b. hope to achieve similar things in life?
   c. not care if they set higher goals for themselves than you do?

9. When people are late for appointments, do you:
   a. get angry and stressed out?
   b. remember that you are sometimes late, too?
   c. not worry, because you are usually late, too?

10. When people are talking to you, do you:
   a. not listen and think about other things?
   b. listen and participate in the conversation?
   c. let them talk and agree with everything they say?

11. When people are expressing their ideas and opinions, do you:
   a. respond and give your own opinions?
   b. listen and sometimes share your own ideas?
   c. listen but not add your own opinions?

SCORING

Count how many a, b, and c answers your partner has. If there are . . .

more a answers: This person is a superachiever.

more b answers: This person is the cool and steady type.

more c answers: This person is the easygoing or carefree type.

B GROUP WORK Compare your scores. Then suggest four characteristics of each personality type.

"The superachiever is the kind of person who . . . . He or she can't stand it when . . . "

A **PAIR WORK** Imagine you and your partner are professional party planners and have been hired to organize an important dinner party. Read about each person on the guest list.

Joanie Van Buren is 42, single, and the host of the party. Wealthy and sociable, she is an art museum volunteer. She has never been married and is rarely seen without her beloved dog.

John Pradesh is 28, single, and a computer software company owner. He was recently voted "Most Promising Entrepreneur" by *Tech* magazine. He puts his career ahead of dating and marriage.

Madge Mathers is 45, married, and a gossip columnist. She's nosy, talkative, and likes to dominate the conversation. She has a good sense of humor and is Joanie's oldest friend.

Buck Eubanks is 54, a widower, and an oil tycoon. This millionaire is bossy and straightforward. His companies have been accused of destroying land to make money.

Emma Smart is 30, single, and a nuclear physicist. She's currently working on top-secret military projects. She's shy, introverted, and recently broke up with her boyfriend of four years.

Pierre is 25, single, and Joanie's favorite chef. He's friendly and ambitious, but can be very moody. He's coming to the party to get celebrities and powerful business executives to invest in his new restaurant.

Sebastiana Di Matteo is 23, single, and a world-famous movie star. She's secretly engaged to her costar in her new movie, and is often followed by photographers.

Ralph Larson is 32, married, and a "green" politician. He's egotistical, outspoken, and tends to start arguments. He's running for public office on an environmental platform.

B **PAIR WORK** Discuss the possible seating arrangements for the party. Then complete this seating plan.

A: Let's seat Buck next to Pierre. Pierre is interested in finding investors for his new restaurant.

B: It might be better to put Buck next to Joanie. He's a widower and she's single, so . . .

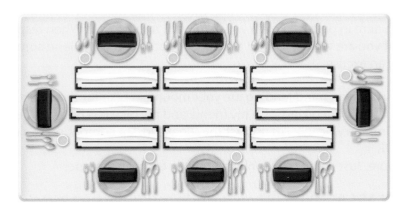

A Imagine you own these items. Which ones would you be willing to lend to a friend? Which ones wouldn't you lend? Check (✓) a response for each item.

mountain bike

☐ wouldn't mind lending
☐ wouldn't want to lend

gold watch

☐ wouldn't mind lending
☐ wouldn't want to lend

hairbrush

☐ wouldn't mind lending
☐ wouldn't want to lend

sleeping bag

☐ wouldn't mind lending
☐ wouldn't want to lend

beach house

☐ wouldn't mind lending
☐ wouldn't want to lend

homework

☐ wouldn't mind lending
☐ wouldn't want to lend

sports car

☐ wouldn't mind lending
☐ wouldn't want to lend

cell phone

☐ wouldn't mind lending
☐ wouldn't want to lend

leather jacket

☐ wouldn't mind lending
☐ wouldn't want to lend

B **CLASS ACTIVITY** Go around the class and take turns asking to borrow each item in part A. Explain why you want to borrow it. When responding, say if you are willing to lend the item or not. If you won't lend something, give an excuse.

A: Would you mind lending me your mountain bike for the weekend?
   I want to go biking with my friend, and my bike has two flat tires.
B: Um, sorry, I can't. I'm using it this weekend. I'm competing in a race.
   OR
B: Sure. Just come over tonight, and you can ride it home.

C **CLASS ACTIVITY** Who was able to borrow the most items?

A DOUBLE ENDING

A Read the beginning and the two possible endings of this story.

Beginning

Ken Passell grew up in a small, working-class family in Detroit, Michigan. His father was an auto mechanic and  his mother worked in a factory. When Ken was a child, he was very good with his hands.

Ending 1

The wedding was the biggest in the history of Los Angeles. After the ceremony, Ken and Cindy left on their private yacht for a honeymoon cruise to Baja, Mexico. When they return, they will live in their twenty-room mansion in Beverly Hills.

Ending 2

Ken and his wife, Cindy, were arrested in London last week. Police found more than $250,000 in cash in their suitcase. The couple insists they are innocent. "I don't know how the money got in our luggage," Ken told the police.

B PAIR WORK Choose one of the endings. What do you think happened during the middle part of the story? Discuss and take notes.

C GROUP WORK Tell your story to another pair. Answer any follow-up questions they have.

A These statements are generally true about cultural behavior in the United States. Check (✓) those that are true in your country.

✓ Comparing Cultures

Find out how typical U.S. cultural behavior compares to yours!

Socializing

☐ 1. Women often kiss their friends on the cheek when they meet.

☐ 2. It's not acceptable to ask people how much money they earn.

☐ 3. People avoid asking each other about their religious beliefs.

☐ 4. When invited to someone's home, people usually arrive on time or a little late.

☐ 5. It's good to ask before bringing a friend or a family member to a party at someone's home.

☐ 6. When someone moves into a new home, it's the custom to give a "housewarming" gift.

☐ 7. People usually call first before dropping by a friend's house.

☐ 8. When eating in a restaurant, friends either split the cost of the meal or take turns paying.

In public

☐ 9. It's OK to blow your nose quietly in public.

☐ 10. It's uncommon to bargain when you buy things in stores.

At work and school

☐ 11. In an office, people usually prefer to be called by their first names.

☐ 12. Students remain seated when the teacher enters the classroom.

Dating and marriage

☐ 13. Teenagers go out on dates.

☐ 14. People decide for themselves who they will marry.

☐ 15. When a couple gets married, the bride's family usually pays for the wedding and the reception.

B **PAIR WORK** Compare your answers with a partner. For the statements you didn't check, why do you think these behaviors are different in your country?

Student A

A Look at this apartment. What's wrong with it? First, make a list of as many problems as you can find in each room.

B **PAIR WORK** Compare your lists. What are the similarities and differences in the problems between your picture here and your partner's picture? Ask questions to find the differences.

A: What's wrong in the living room?
B: Well, in my picture, the sofa has a hole in it. And the carpet . . .
A: Oh, really? In my picture, the sofa has a hole in it, but the carpet . . . , and the wallpaper . . .

Student B

A Look at this apartment. What's wrong with it? First, make a list of as many problems as you can find in each room.

B **PAIR WORK** Compare your lists. What are the similarities and differences in the problems between your picture here and your partner's picture? Ask questions to find the differences.

A: What's wrong in the living room?
B: Well, in my picture, the sofa has a hole in it. And the carpet . . .
A: Oh, really? In my picture, the sofa has a hole in it, but the carpet . . . , and the wallpaper . . .

A Read about these issues. Which one would you most likely protest?

> Starting next month, local transit authorities will raise the cost of all public transportation in and around your city. | Gove͏
> ͏uth͏

> A popular soda company has been secretly using addictive and potentially harmful chemicals in its recipe to increase sales.

> The government is negotiating the sale of portions of your country's biggest wildlife preserve to an oil-drilling company. | T
> r

B **GROUP WORK** Find other students who chose the same issue. Then look at these methods of protest. Which are the most effective for the issue you chose? Complete the chart.

a demonstration

a sit-in

a petition

Method of protest	Very effective	Somewhat effective	Not effective
organize a demonstration	☐	☐	☐
start an email writing campaign	☐	☐	☐
stage a sit-in	☐	☐	☐
boycott a product or a service	☐	☐	☐
ask people to sign a petition	☐	☐	☐
pay for ads on TV or the radio	☐	☐	☐
use social networking to gather support	☐	☐	☐
call your local government representative	☐	☐	☐
distribute pamphlets about the issue	☐	☐	☐
hold an awareness campaign in schools	☐	☐	☐

Develop a strategy to make your voices heard using the above methods or your own ideas.

C **CLASS ACTIVITY** How did you decide to deal with the issue? Present your group's strategy to the class.

A Complete this chart with information about yourself. Add one idea of your own.

two foreign languages I'd like to speak	....	....
two musical instruments I'd like to play	....	....
two dances I'd like to learn	....	....
two types of cuisine I'd like to learn how to cook	....	....
two evening courses I'd like to take	....	....
two sports I'd like to play	....	....
two skills that I'd like to improve	....	....
two	....	....

B **CLASS ACTIVITY** Ask three classmates to help you choose between the things you wrote down in part A. Write their recommendations in the chart.

Names:	....	....	....
foreign language	....	....	....
musical instrument	....	....	....
dance	....	....	....
cuisine	....	....	....
evening course	....	....	....
sport	....	....	....
skill	....	....	....
....	....	....	....

A: I don't know if I'd rather learn Portuguese or Turkish. What do you think?

B: Hmm. If I were you, I'd learn Portuguese.

A: Why Portuguese and not Turkish?

B: Well, you already know Spanish, so Portuguese might be easier to learn.

C **GROUP WORK** What are your final choices? Who gave the best advice? Why?

PUT YOURSELF IN MY SHOES!

A **PAIR WORK** Read these comments made by parents. Why do you think they feel this way? Think of two arguments to support each point of view.

Our daughter wants to get her ears pierced. We think she should wait until she's 16.

Our son wants to get his computer upgraded, but it's not necessary. We just bought it last year!

If our daughter insists on having her nails done, she has to pay for it herself.

Our son wants to buy a motorcycle. He has the money, but we feel he should save it for college.

Our daughter wants to go to a rock concert with her friends. Absolutely not!

Our son wants to have his hair cut at an expensive salon. What's wrong with a regular barber?

Regardless of the color, we refuse to let our kids get their hair dyed.

A: Why do you think they won't let their daughter get her ears pierced?
B: They probably think she's too young.
A: They may also feel that she . . .

B **PAIR WORK** Now put yourselves in the children's shoes. One of you is the daughter and the other is the son. Discuss the parents' decisions, and think of two arguments against their point of view.

A: Why do you think mom and dad won't let me get my ears pierced?
B: They probably think you're too young.
A: That's crazy! My friend got her ears pierced when she was 10. It's not a big deal.

C **CLASS ACTIVITY** Take a vote. Do you agree with the parents or the children? Why?

Student A

A **PAIR WORK** Ask your partner these questions. Put a check (✓) if your partner gives the correct answer. (The correct answers are in **bold**.)

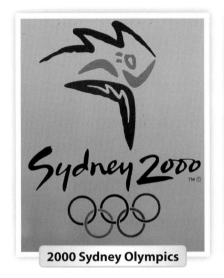

2000 Sydney Olympics

3D movie from the 1950s

Cleopatra

Test Your Knowledge

1. Was Julius Caesar emperor of Athens, **Rome**, or Constantinople?

2. What did Thomas Edison invent in 1879? Was it the television, the telephone, or the **lightbulb**?

3. In which year did Mexico gain its independence? Was it in 1721, **1821**, or 1921?

4. Where were the 2000 Olympics held? Were they in Athens, **Sydney**, or Beijing?

5. When did World War I take place? Was it from 1898 to 1903, from 1911 to 1915, or **from 1914 to 1918**?

6. What sculptor made the famous statue of David? Was it Leonardo da Vinci, Auguste Bartholdi, or **Michelangelo**?

7. Who was the first human in space? Was it **Yuri Gagarin**, Neil Armstrong, or John Glenn?

8. When were the first audio CDs put on the market? Was it in 1973, **1983**, or 1993?

9. In what decade did 3-D movies first gain wide popularity? Was it the **1950s**, 1960s, or 1970s?

10. Was Cleopatra the queen of **Egypt**, Rome, or Greece?

B **PAIR WORK** Answer the questions your partner asks you. Then compare quizzes. Who has the most correct answers?

C **CLASS ACTIVITY** Think of three more questions of your own. Can the rest of the class answer them?

WHEN I WAS YOUNGER, . . .

A PAIR WORK Play the board game. Follow these instructions.

1. Use small pieces of paper with your initials on them as markers.
2. Take turns by tossing a coin:

 Heads Move two spaces.   **Tails** Move one space.

3. When you land on a space, tell your partner what is true. Then say how things would have been different. For example:

"When I was younger, I didn't pay attention in class. If I had paid attention in class, I would have gotten better grades."
OR
"When I was younger, I paid attention in class. If I hadn't paid attention in class, I wouldn't have won a scholarship."

B CLASS ACTIVITY Who was sensible when they were younger?
Who was rebellious? Tell the class.

Student B

A **PAIR WORK** Answer the questions your partner asks you.

B **PAIR WORK** Ask your partner these questions. Put a check (✓) if your partner gives the correct answer. (The correct answers are in **bold**.) Then compare quizzes. Who has the most correct answers?

The Wright Brothers

Mary Shelley's *Frankenstein*

Hong Kong, 1997

Test Your Knowledge ✓

1. When did the Wright brothers make their first airplane flight? Was it in 1893, **1903**, or 1923?

2. What was the former name of New York City? Was it New England, New London, or **New Amsterdam**?

3. When did Walt Disney make his first cartoon movie? Was it in 1920, **1938**, or 1947?

4. In which century did the composer Mozart live? Was it the seventeenth, **eighteenth**, or nineteenth century?

5. Who was the novel *Frankenstein* written by? Was it Jane Austen, John Keats, or **Mary Shelley**?

6. Who discovered penicillin? Was it **Alexander Fleming**, Marie Curie, or Albert Einstein?

7. When was the first Volkswagen "Beetle" car built? Was it during the 1920s, the **1930s**, or the 1940s?

8. Who used the first magnetic compass? Was it the Portuguese, **the Chinese**, or the Dutch?

9. When did the British return Hong Kong to China? Was it in 1995, 1996, or **1997**?

10. Was the theory of relativity created by **Albert Einstein**, Charles Darwin, or Isaac Newton?

C **CLASS ACTIVITY** Think of three more questions of your own. Can the rest of the class answer them?

A PAIR WORK Read these popular slogans for products.
Match the slogans with the product types.

1. It's the real thing. ....
2. The happiest place on earth ....
3. Good to the last drop ....
4. All the news that's fit to print ....
5. Just do it! ....
6. Bet you can't eat just one. ....

a. an amusement park
b. a soft drink
c. coffee
d. a daily newspaper
e. potato chips
f. sports clothing

7. You're in good hands. ....
8. Reach out and touch someone. ....
9. Alarmed? You should be. ....
10. M'm! M'm! Good! ....
11. Built for the road ahead ....
12. Have it your way. ....

g. fast food
h. automobiles
i. security systems
j. insurance
k. soup
l. telephone service

B PAIR WORK Join another pair and compare your answers.
Then check your answers at the bottom of the page.

C GROUP WORK Think of a product. Then create your
own slogan for it and add a logo. Consider a design
and colors that are suitable for the product.

A: Any idea for a product?
B: What about a pizza delivery service?
C: That's good. Let's try to think of some catchy slogans.
D: How about "Delicious and dependable"? Or maybe . . .

D CLASS ACTIVITY Present your slogans to the class.
Who has the catchiest one?

Answers: 1. b; 2. a; 3. c; 4. d; 5. f; 6. e; 7. j; 8. l; 9. i; 10. k; 11. h; 12. g

A **PAIR WORK** Look at these pictures. What do you think might have happened in each situation? Talk about possibilities for each picture.

A: Maybe the woman thought of something funny that had happened earlier.
B: Or, she might not have understood . . .

B **GROUP WORK** Agree on one interpretation of each situation and share it with the class. Be ready to answer any questions.

A GROUP WORK Here are some additional jobs in the movie industry.
What do you think each person does?

art director   costume designer   makeup artist   sound-effects technician
cinematographer   lighting technician   set designer   special-effects designer

A: What does an art director do?
B: I know. An art director manages the people who build the sets.

B GROUP WORK Imagine you are going to make a movie. What kind of
movie will it be? Decide what job each person in your group will do.

A: You should be the art director because you're a good leader.
B: Actually, I'd prefer to be the producer.
C: I think I'd like to be one of the actors.

C CLASS ACTIVITY Tell the class what kind of movie you are going to make.
Explain how each person will contribute to the making of the film.

a cinematographer

a makeup artist

a lighting technician

a sound-effects technician

A **PAIR WORK** What punishment (if any) is appropriate for each possible offense? Complete the chart.

Offense	Punishment
1. failing to clean up after a dog	....
2. crossing the street in dangerous places	....
3. leaving trash on public streets	....
4. using a cell phone while driving	....
5. buying pirated DVDs and video games	....
6. driving without a seat belt	....
7. riding a motorcycle without a helmet	....
8. painting graffiti on public property	....
9. stealing from your company	....
10. shoplifting	....
11. hacking into a government computer	....
12.	....
(your own idea)	

A: What do you think should be done about people who don't clean up after their dogs?
B: They should be required to pay a fine.
A: I don't agree. I think . . .

possible punishments

receive a warning
spend some time in jail
pay a fine
lose a driver's license
get suspended
do community service

B **GROUP WORK** Join another pair of students. Then compare and discuss your lists. Do you agree or disagree? Try to convince each other that you are right!

A Complete this survey with your viewpoints on communities, charities, and volunteering.

WHAT DO YOU THINK?

1 **Do you help out in your community?**
- ⊝ Yes, I do regularly.
- ⊝ Yes, I do from time to time.
- ⊝ No, I don't right now.
- ⊝ other: _____

2 **Would you consider working in a developing country?**
- ⊝ Yes. It would be an interesting experience.
- ⊝ Maybe when I'm older.
- ⊝ No. That's definitely not for me.
- ⊝ other: _____

3 **What's the best way to raise money for charities?**
- ⊝ through donations
- ⊝ through taxes
- ⊝ through special fund-raising activities
- ⊝ other: _____

4 **Who do you think has the greatest responsibility to support charities?**
- ⊝ the government
- ⊝ all citizens
- ⊝ the wealthy
- ⊝ other: _____

5 **What's the best way to improve a community?**
- ⊝ through education
- ⊝ by creating more jobs
- ⊝ by protecting the environment
- ⊝ other: _____

6 **Which of these things are you most concerned about?**
- ⊝ the environment
- ⊝ crime and safety
- ⊝ unemployment
- ⊝ other: _____

7 **Which of these activities would you prefer doing?**
- ⊝ helping the elderly
- ⊝ helping the poor
- ⊝ helping the sick
- ⊝ other: _____

8 **What advice would you give someone who wanted to work for a charitable organization?**
- ⊝ Go for it! It can be very rewarding.
- ⊝ Be selective about who you decide to work for.
- ⊝ Don't do it. It's a waste of time.
- ⊝ other: _____

B **PAIR WORK** Compare your responses. Do you and your partner have similar viewpoints?

C **CLASS ACTIVITY** Take a class poll. Which choice was the most popular for each question? Talk about any "other" responses people added.

Grammar plus

Unit 1

1 Relative pronouns (page 3)

> ▶ A relative pronoun – *who* or *that* – is necessary when the pronoun is the subject of the clause: I'd love to meet someone **who/that** is considerate. (NOT: I'd love to meet ~~someone is considerate.~~)
> ▶ When the pronoun is the object of the clause, *who* and *that* can be left out: I'd like a roommate **who/that** I have a lot in common with. OR I'd like a roommate I have a lot in common with.

Complete the conversation with *who* or *that*. Put an **X** when a relative pronoun isn't necessary.

A: Ana, have you met Clint – the guy ....**X**........ Laurie is going to marry?

B: Oh, Clint and I have been friends for years. In fact, I'm the one .... introduced Laurie and Clint.

A: Do you think they're right for each other?

B: Definitely. They're two people .... have a lot in common – but not *too* much.

A: What does that mean?

B: Well, you don't want a partner .... doesn't have his or her own interests. Couples .... do everything together usually don't last very long.

A: I guess you're right, but the opposite isn't good, either. My last girlfriend was someone .... I had nothing in common with. She wasn't the kind of girl .... I could talk to easily.

B: Well, you can talk to *me* easily. . . .

2 *It* clauses + adverbial clauses with *when* (page 6)

> ▶ In sentences with an *it* clause + an adverbial clause with *when*, the word *it* refers to and means the same as the adverbial clause with *when*. The *it* in these sentences is necessary and cannot be left out: I hate **it when** people talk on a cell phone in an elevator. (NOT: I ~~hate when~~ people . . .) **It** bothers me **when** people talk on a cell phone in an elevator. (NOT: ~~Bothers~~ me when people . . .)

Rewrite the sentences using the words in parentheses.

1. I can't stand it when people call me before 8:00 A.M. (it really bothers me)
   It really bothers me when people call me before 8:00 a.m.

2. It upsets me when I don't have enough time to study for an exam. (I hate it)
   ....

3. I don't mind it when friends talk to me about their problems. (it doesn't bother me)
   ....

4. I don't like it when I forget a co-worker's name. (it embarrasses me)
   ....

5. It makes me happy when my friends send me emails. (I love it)
   ....

6. I hate it when I have to wait for someone. (it upsets me)
   ....

Unit 2

1 Gerund phrases (page 9)

> ▶ A gerund phrase as a subject takes a singular verb: Taking care of children **is** a rewarding job. (NOT: Taking care of children ~~are~~ a rewarding job.)
>
> ▶ There are some common verb + preposition expressions (for example, *dream about, feel like, talk about, think about*) and adjective + preposition phrases (for example, *good/bad at, excited by/about, interested in, tired of, used to*) that are followed by a gerund: I'm **thinking about looking for** a new job. I'm **tired of working** long hours.

Complete the sentences with the correct gerund forms of the verbs in the box.

✓ become	have	make	stand	travel
change	learn	solve	take	work

1. My brother's very interested in ..*becoming*.. a flight attendant. He dreams about .... to new places.
2. I'm excited about .... a Japanese class next semester. I enjoy .... languages.
3. You wouldn't like .... in a restaurant. You'd get tired of .... on your feet throughout the long shifts!
4. Our teacher is very good at .... problems. Maybe she should think about .... careers to become a guidance counselor.
5. .... a living as a photographer could be challenging. .... an impressive portfolio is really important to attract new clients and employers.

2 Comparisons (page 11)

> ▶ When making general comparisons with count nouns, use *a/an* + singular noun or no article + plural noun: **A pilot** earns more than **a flight attendant**. **Pilots** earn more than **flight attendants**. (NOT: ~~The~~ pilots earn more than ~~the~~ flight attendants.)

Make comparisons with the information below. Add articles and other words necessary.

1. architect / more education / hairstylist
   An architect needs more education than a hairstylist.
2. college professor / earn more / elementary school teacher
   ....
3. nurses / worse hours / psychiatrists
   ....
4. working as a police officer / as dangerous / being a firefighter
   ....
5. taxi driver / not as well paid / electrician
   ....
6. being a tour guide / less interesting / being an actor
   ....

Unit 3

1 Requests with modals, *if* clauses, and gerunds (page 17)

> ▶ Use the simple past form – not the gerund or simple present form – after *if* with *Would you mind . . . ?* and *Would it be all right . . . ?*: **Would you mind if I used** your car? **Would it be all right if I used** your car? (NOT: Would you mind if I ~~using~~ your car? OR Would it be all right if I ~~use~~ your car?)

Read the situations. Then complete the requests.

1. You want to borrow a friend's underwater camera for a diving trip.
    A: I was wondering *if I could borrow your underwater camera.*
    B: Sure. That's fine. Just please be careful with it.
2. You want to use your roommate's computer.
    A: Is it OK
    B: You can use it, but please save my work first.
3. Your neighbor has a car. You need a ride to class.
    A: Would you mind
    B: I'd be glad to. What time should I pick you up?
4. You want your brother to help you move on Saturday.
    A: Can you
    B: I'm sorry. I'm busy all weekend.
5. You would like a second piece of your aunt's cherry pie.
    A: Would it be all right
    B: Yes, of course! Just pass me your plate.
6. You want to borrow your cousin's red sweater.
    A: Could you
    B: Sorry. I don't like it when other people wear my clothes.

2 Indirect requests (page 20)

> ▶ In indirect requests with negative infinitives, *not* comes before – not between – the infinitive: Could you tell Allie **not to be** late? (NOT: Could you tell Allie ~~to not be~~ late?)

Complete the indirect requests. Ask someone to deliver the messages to Susie.

1. Are you busy this weekend? → Could *you ask Susie if she's busy this weekend?*
2. Do you want to hang out with me? → Can
3. Email me. → Can
4. Do you know my address? → Can
5. Don't forget to write. → Could
6. What are you doing Saturday? → Can
7. Do you have plans on Sunday? → Could

Unit 4

1 Past continuous vs. simple past (page 23)

▶ Verbs for non-actions or states are rarely used in the past continuous: I **wanted** to stop, but I couldn't. (NOT: I ~~was wanting~~ to stop . . .)

Circle the best forms to complete the conversations.

1. A: How **did you break** / were you breaking your arm?
   B: It's a crazy story! Ramon and I **rode** / **were riding** our bikes in the park when a cat **ran** / **was running** out in front of me. I **went** / **was going** pretty fast, so when I **tried** / **was trying** to stop, I **went** / **was going** off the road and **fell** / **was falling**.
   A: That's terrible! **Did you go** / **Were you going** to the hospital after it **happened** / **was happening**?
   B: Yes. Luckily, we **weren't** / **weren't being** too far from City Hospital, so we **went** / **were going** there.
2. A: You'll never guess what **happened** / **was happening** to me this morning!
   B: What?
   A: Well, I **brushed** / **was brushing** my teeth when suddenly the water **went** / **was going** off. I **had** / **was having** toothpaste all over my mouth, and I couldn't wash it out.
   B: So what **did you do** / **were you doing**?
   A: Fortunately, I **had** / **was having** a big bottle of water in the refrigerator, so I **used** / **was using** that water to rinse my mouth.

2 Past perfect (page 25)

▶ Use the past perfect to show that one past action happened before another past action: I **wasn't able to** pay for lunch because I **had left** my wallet at work.

PAST _____X_____X_____ NOW
          had left   wasn't able
          my wallet   to pay

Combine the two ideas into one with a past event and a past perfect event. Use *when* or *because*.

1. The museum closed. A thief stole a famous painting earlier.
   The museum closed because a thief had stolen a famous painting earlier.
2. We finished cleaning the house. Then our guests arrived.
   ....
3. Someone robbed my house yesterday. I left the window open.
   ....
4. There was no food in the house. We forgot to stop at the supermarket.
   ....
5. I called her three times. She finally answered.
   ....
6. I knew about the problem. Your brother told me about it.
   ....

Unit 5

1 Noun phrases containing relative clauses (page 31)

▶ The relative pronoun *who* or *that* can be left out in noun phrases as subjects and as objects. These four sentences have exactly the same meaning: One thing I'd be nervous about is getting lost. One thing that I'd be nervous about is getting lost. Getting lost is one thing I'd be nervous about. Getting lost is one thing that I'd be nervous about.

Answer the questions using the words in parentheses. Write each sentence two ways. Leave out the relative pronouns.

If you went to live in a foreign country, . . .

1. Who would you miss a lot? (person: my best friend)
   a. One person I'd miss a lot is my best friend.
   b. My best friend is one person I'd miss a lot.
2. What would you be very interested in? (things: the food and the music)
   a. ....
   b. ....
3. What would you be worried about? (something: not understanding the customs)
   a. ....
   b. ....
4. Who would you stay in touch with? (people: my brother and sister)
   a. ....
   b. ....
5. What would you feel insecure about? (thing: speaking a new language)
   a. ....
   b. ....

2 Expectations (page 33)

▶ Use the base form of a verb – not the gerund – after these expressions for expectations: *be the custom to, be supposed to, be expected to, be acceptable to*: It's the custom to **arrive** a little late. (NOT: It's the custom to ~~arriving~~ a little late.)

Complete the sentences with the clauses in the box.

> it's not acceptable to show up without calling first
> it's the custom for them to sit across from each other
> you're expected to reply within a few days
> you're supposed to bring a gift.
> ✓ you're supposed to shake his or her hand

1. When you meet someone for the first time, you're supposed to shake his or her hand.
2. When a friend sends you an email, ...
3. If you want to visit someone, ...
4. If you invite a married couple to dinner, ...
5. When you go to a birthday party, ...

Unit 6

1 Describing problems 1 (page 37)

▶ The simple past and the past participle of regular verbs are the same: I **chipped** the vase. The vase is **chipped**. BUT Many irregular verbs have different simple past and past participle forms: I **tore** my jacket. My jacket is **torn**.

Complete the conversations with the correct words from the box.

are stained	has a dent	✓have a tear	is broken	is scratched
has a chip	has a stain	is a hole	is leaking	some damage

1. A: Oh, no! These jeans ......*have a tear*...... in them.
   B: And they .... , too.
2. A: This table has .... on top.
   B: I know. The wood .... because my son drags his toy cars on it.
3. A: Why are you drinking out of that glass? It .... in it.
   B: Oh, I didn't see it. That's why it ....
4. A: Someone hit my car today. Look! The door .... in it.
   B: I see that. Your back light .... , too.
5. A: I bought this blouse yesterday, but I have to take it back. There ....
   in it.
   B: It's really cute, but that's not the only problem. It .... on it, too.

2 Describing problems 2 (page 39)

▶ Use the past participle – not the present participle or gerund – with passive forms: The oven needs to be **fixed**. (NOT: The oven needs to be ~~fixing~~.)

A Complete the conversation with the verbs in parentheses. Use *need* + passive infinitive in A's lines and *need* + gerund in B's lines.

A: Look at this place! A lot of work ......*needs to be done*...... (do) before we move in.
B: You're not kidding. Let's make a list. First, the walls ......*need painting*..... (paint).
A: Right. And the windows .... (wash). Add the rug to
   your list: It really .... (clean). Do you think it ....
   (dry-clean)?
B: No, I think we can do it ourselves. It .... (shampoo).
   We can rent a machine for that.
A: And what about the ceiling fan? I think it .... (replace).
   Fans aren't too expensive.
B: OK. I've added it to the list. And what should we do with all this old furniture?
A: It .... (throw out)! I think the landlord should take care of |
   that, though.

B Complete the blog with the correct form of *keep* and the verb
in parentheses.

I ......*keep having*...... (have) technical problems. My computer
.... (crash), and my printer .... (jam). I have
to .... (put) a new battery into my mouse because it
.... (die). The letters on my keyboard .... (stick),
too. I .... (think) things will get better, but they just
.... (get) worse. Time for some new electronics!

Unit 7

1 Passive with prepositions (page 45)

▶ The prepositions *by, as a result of, because of, through,* and *due to* have similar meanings. They are used in sentences that describe cause and effect; they introduce the cause.

Match phrases from each column to make sentences. (More than one answer may be possible.)

Subject	Effect	Cause
1. The environment	is being contaminated due to	improper disposal of medical waste.
2. Our soil	is being harmed by	deforestation to make paper products.
3. Infectious diseases	are being endangered due to	hybrid cars.
4. Many different species	has been affected because of	the use of pesticides on fruits and vegetables.
5. Our air quality	has been reduced as a result of	the destruction of their habitats.
6. Smog pollution	have been spread through	climate changes like global warming.

2 Infinitive clauses and phrases (page 47)

▶ The form of *be* that follows the first infinitive must agree with the subject: The best way to reduce pollution **is** to improve public transportation. BUT The best ways to reduce homelessness **are** to build more public housing and provide free health care.

A Match the phrases.

1. What are the best ways to make ....e....
2. And the best way to do that is ....
3. The best ways to reduce ....
4. One way to improve ....
5. Another way to make ....

a. people happier is to make the air healthier.
b. to create a larger police force.
c. people's quality of life is to help them feel safe.
d. air pollution are to ban cars and control industry.
e. this city a better place to live?

B Complete the conversation with the sentences above.

A: What are the best ways to make this city a better place to live? ....
B: Well, ...
A: That's right. ....
B: I agree. ....
A: Yes. Good air quality is key. ....
B: Maybe it's time to share our ideas with the mayor. Hand me my laptop.

Unit 8

1 *Would rather* and *would prefer* (page 51)

▶ In negative statements with *would rather* and *would prefer*, the word *not* comes after the verbs: I**'d rather not**/I**'d prefer not** to take any courses this semester. (NOT: I ~~wouldn't rather~~/I ~~wouldn't prefer~~ to . . .)

Write questions and responses using the words in parentheses.

1. A: <u>Would you prefer to take classes during the day or at night?</u>
   (prefer / take classes / during the day / at night)
   B: ....
   (rather / take classes / at night)
2. A: ....
   (rather / study / business / education)
   B: ....
   (prefer / major in / education)
3. A: ....
   (prefer / sign up for / a biology course / an engineering course)
   B: ....
   (rather / not / take / either)
4. A: ....
   (rather / take / computer science / history)
   B: ....
   (prefer / not / take / a class this semester)

2 *By* + gerund to describe how to do things (page 53)

▶ In negative sentences that express comparison with *by* + gerund and *but*, *not* comes before *by*: A good way to improve your accent is **not by watching** TV **but by talking** to native speakers. In negative sentences with *by* that give advice without a comparison, *not* comes after *by*: A good way to improve your accent is **by not imitating** non-native speakers.

Combine the two ideas into one sentence using *by* + gerund.

1. There is a good way to learn idioms. Learners can watch American movies.
   <u>A good way to learn idioms is by watching American movies.</u>
2. You can build your vocabulary. Write down new words and expressions.
   ....
3. Students can improve their listening skills. They can listen to English-language radio.
   ....
4. Hardworking students improve their grammar. They don't repeat common mistakes.
   ....
5. You can become fluent. Don't translate everything. Try to think in English.
   ....
6. You can become a good conversationalist. Don't just talk with others. Talk to yourself when you're alone, too.
   ....

Unit 9

1 Get or have something done (page 59)

▶ Sentences with *get/have* + object + past participle are passive. BUT Don't use any form of *be* before the past participle: Where can I **have** my watch **fixed**? (NOT: Where can I have my watch ~~be~~ fixed?)

Rewrite the statements as questions with *Where can I get/have ... ?* Then complete B's answers with the information in parentheses.

1. I want to have someone shorten this skirt.
   A: *Where can I have this skirt shortened?*
   B: *You can have it shortened at Cathy's Cleaners.* (at Cathy's Cleaners)
2. I need to get someone to repair my computer.
   A: ....
   B: .... (at Hackers Inc.)
3. I need to have someone prepare my taxes.
   A: ....
   B: .... (by my accountant)
4. I'd like to get someone to cut my hair.
   A: ....
   B: .... (at Beauty Barn)
5. I need to have someone paint my apartment.
   A: ....
   B: .... (by Peter the Painter)

2 Making suggestions (page 61)

▶ Use the base form of a verb – without *to* – after *Maybe you could ...* and *Why don't you ... ?*: Maybe you could **join** a book club. (NOT: Maybe you could ~~to~~ join a book club.) Why don't you **join** a book club? (NOT: Why don't you ~~to~~ join a book club?)

Complete the conversations with the correct form of the verbs in parentheses.

A: I'm having trouble meeting people here in the city. Any ideas?
B: I know it's hard. Why don't you ....*join*.... (join) a gym? That's usually a good place to meet people. Or maybe you could .... (take) a class at the community college.
A: What about .... (check out) the personal ads? Do you think that's a good way to meet people?
B: I wouldn't recommend doing that. People never tell the truth in those ads. But it might be a good idea .... (find) a sports team. Have you thought about .... (play) a team sport – maybe baseball or volleyball?
A: I'm not very good at most sports, but I used to play tennis.
B: There you go! One option is .... (look up) tennis clubs in the city and see which clubs have teams people can join.
A: Now, that's a great idea. And I could always use the exercise!

Unit 10

1 Referring to time in the past (page 65)

> ▶ Use *since* with a particular time: The UN has been in existence **since** 1945. Use *for* with a duration of time: The UN has been in existence **for** about the last 70 years.
> ▶ Use *in* and *during* with a specific period of time: Rock 'n' roll became popular **in/during** the 1950s.
> ▶ Use *from* and *to* to describe when something began and ended: World War II lasted **from** 1939 **to** 1945.

Complete the conversation with the words in the box. (Use some of the words more than once.)

| ago | during | for | from | in | since | to |

A: Hey, Dad. Did you use to listen to the Beatles?

B: Of course. In fact, I just listened to one of their records a few days ......*ago*...... . Do you realize that the Beatles' music has influenced other musicians .... over 50 years? They were the greatest!

A: Well, I just found some interesting information about them. I'll read it to you: "The Beatles were a well-known British band .... the 1960s. They performed together .... ten years – .... 1960 .... 1970. .... 2003, the Beatles released another album, even though one of the original members had been dead .... 1980 and another had died .... 2001. The album had been recorded .... 1969 and was in the studio safe .... 34 years before it was released."

B: That *is* interesting. It's pretty amazing that people have listened to the Beatles .... both the twentieth and the twenty-first centuries, isn't it?

2 Predicting the future with *will* (page 67)

> ▶ In sentences referring to time, the preposition *by* means "not later than." Don't confuse *by* with *within*, which means "some time during." Use *by* with points in time; use *within* with periods of time: **By** 2050, we will have eliminated starvation around the world. (NOT: ~~Within~~ 2050, . . .) **Within** the next five years, people will have invented mobile phone applications for nearly everything! (NOT: ~~By~~ the next five years, . . .)

Circle the correct verb forms to complete the conversation.

A: What do you think you **will do** / (**will be doing**) five years from now?

B: I'm not sure. Maybe I **will get** / **will have gotten** married by then. How about you?

A: I **will be finishing** / **will have finished** medical school, so I **will be doing** / **will have done** my internship five years from now.

B: So you **won't be living** / **won't have lived** around here in five years, I guess. Where do you think you **will live** / **will have lived**?

A: Wherever I get my internship.

Unit 11

1 Time clauses (page 73)

▶ Use the past perfect in the main clause with *until* and *by the time*. This shows that one of the past events happened before the other: Until I got my driver's license, I **had** always **taken** public transportation. By the time I got my driver's license, all of my friends **had** already **gotten** theirs.

Circle the correct time expression to complete each sentence.

1. **After /** (**Until**) I traveled overseas, I hadn't known much about different cultures.
2. **After / Before** I got a full-time job, I had to live on a very limited budget.
3. **By the time / Once** I finished high school, I had already taken three college courses.
4. **As soon as / Before** I left for college, my mother turned my room into her office.
5. **Once / Until** I left home, I realized how much my family meant to me.
6. **By the time / The moment** you have a child, you feel totally responsible for him or her.

2 Expressing regret and describing hypothetical situations (page 75)

▶ Conditional sentences describing hypothetical situations often refer to both the present and the past:
If I**'d finished** college, I**'d have** a better job now.
    past   present
(NOT: If I'd finished college, I'd ~~have had~~ a better job now.)

A Write sentences with *should (not) have* to express regret about each person's situation.

1. Sarah was very argumentative with her teacher, so she had to stay after school.
   Sarah shouldn't have been argumentative with her teacher.

2. Ivan didn't save up for a car, so he still has to take public transportation.
   ....

3. Jon was very inactive when he was in college, so he gained a lot of weight.
   ....

4. Lisa didn't stay in touch with her high school classmates, so now she has very few friends.
   ....

5. Tony didn't study Spanish in school, so he's not bilingual now.
   ....

B Rewrite your sentences in Exercise A, changing them to hypothetical situations.

1. If Sarah hadn't been argumentative with her teacher, she wouldn't have had to stay after school.

2. ....
   ....

3. ....
   ....

4. ....
   ....

5. ....
   ....

Unit 12

1 Describing purpose (page 79)

▶ Don't use *for* immediately before an infinitive: **To have** a successful business, you need a lot of luck. (NOT: ~~For~~ to have a successful business, you need a lot of luck.)

A Complete the sentences with *in order to* or *in order for*.

1. ....*In order for*.... a supermarket to succeed, it has to be clean and well organized.
2. .... stay popular, a website needs to be accurate and visually attractive.
3. .... run a profitable furniture store, it's important to advertise on TV.
4. .... a restaurant to stay in business, it needs to have "regulars" – customers that come often.
5. .... establish a successful nail salon, it has to have a convenient location.
6. .... an online business to survive, it's a good idea to have excellent pictures of the merchandise it's selling.

B Rewrite the sentences in Exercise A without *In order*.

1. ...*For a supermarket to succeed, it has to be clean and well organized.*...
2. ....
3. ....
4. ....
5. ....
6. ....

2 Giving reasons (page 81)

▶ *Because* and *since* have the same meaning, and they can begin or end a sentence: **Because/Since** the food is always fantastic, Giorgio's is my favorite restaurant. = Giorgio's is my favorite restaurant **because/since** the food is always fantastic.
▶ Don't confuse *because* and *because of*. *Because* introduces an adverb clause and is followed by a subject and verb, while *because of* is a preposition and is followed by a noun object: **Because** Giorgio's is so popular, we should get there early. Giorgio's is popular **because of** its food and service.

Circle the correct words to complete the conversation.

A: I had to go downtown today **because / because of / due to** I needed to mail a package at the post office. **Due to / For / Since** I was only a few blocks from Main Street, I went over to Martin's. Did you know that Martin's has gone out of business? I'm so upset!

B: That's too bad, but I'm not surprised. A lot of family-owned shops are closing **because / because of / since** the construction of shopping malls.

A: Yeah, and don't forget about all the megastores that are popping up everywhere. **Because / For / The reason why** people prefer to shop there is to save money. Everyone loves a megastore **because / due to / since** the low prices and the huge selection.

B: Not me! I loved Martin's **for / since / the reason that** their beautiful clothes and friendly salespeople. When you were there, you almost felt like family. You'll never get that at a megastore!

Unit 13

1 Past modals for degrees of certainty (page 87)

▶ Use the past modal *could have* to express possibility. BUT Use *couldn't have* when you are almost 100% sure something is impossible: I suppose he **could have gotten** stuck in traffic, but he **couldn't have forgotten** his own birthday party.

Complete the conversations with past modals *must (not) have, could (not) have,* or *may/might (not) have.* Use the degrees of certainty and the verbs in parentheses. (More than one answer may be possible.)

1. A: Yoko still hasn't called me back.
   B: She ....*might not have gotten*.... your message. (it's possible – not get)
2. A: What's wrong with Steven?
   B: Oh, you .... the news. His dog ran away. (it's almost certain – not hear)
3. A: I went to see the Larsens today, but they didn't answer the door.
   B: Was their car there? If so, they .... in the backyard. (it's possible – be)
4. A: Fabio said he was going to the party last night, but I didn't see him.
   B: Neither did I. He .... there then. (it's not possible – not be)
5. A: I can't find my glasses, but I know I had them at work today.
   B: You .... them at the office. (it's possible – leave)
6. A: Marc's new car looks really expensive.
   B: Yes, it does. It .... a fortune! (it's almost certain – cost)

2 Past modals for judgments and suggestions (page 89)

▶ In advice with *would have*, the speaker means, "If I were you, ..."

Read each situation and choose the corresponding judgment or suggestion for an alternative past action.

Situation
1. Sue forgot her boyfriend's birthday. ...*b*...
2. Tim got a speeding ticket. ....
3. Ruth still hasn't paid me back. ....
4. Bill lied to us. ....
5. I spent an hour making Joe dinner, and he didn't even thank me. ....
6. Carol came over for dinner empty-handed. ....

Judgment/Suggestion
a. I wouldn't have lent her money.
b. She should have put it on her calendar.
c. He should have told the truth.
d. He shouldn't have gone over the limit.
e. She should have brought something.
f. I wouldn't have cooked for him.

Unit 14

1 The passive to describe process (page 93)

> ▶ The modals *have to* and *need to* must agree with the subject; other modals, like *may be*, have only one form: Each scene **has to/needs to** be filmed from several different angles.

Put the words in the correct order to make sentences.

1. overnight / business / A / started / small / isn't / .
   A small business isn't started overnight.

2. to / plan / business / a / written / First, / be / has / .
   ....

3. research / Next, / done / be / market / should / .
   ....

4. needs / competition / to / the / Then / identified / be / .
   ....

5. online / ads / posted / be / Classified / may / .
   ....

6. work / are / employees / be / hired / can / started / the / so / Finally, / .
   ....

2 Defining and non-defining relative clauses (page 96)

> ▶ Use either *who* or *that* in defining relative clauses about people: A set designer is an artist **who/that** makes important contributions to a theater production. BUT Use only *who* in non-defining relative clauses about people: A set designer, **who** makes important contributions to a theater production, has to be very creative. (NOT: A set designer, ~~that~~ makes . . .)
> ▶ Use commas before and after a non-defining clause: A gossip columnist**,** who gets to go to fabulous parties**,** writes about celebrities and scandals.

Combine these sentences with *who* or *that*. Add a comma wherever one is necessary.

1. A prop designer makes sure everything on a movie set looks realistic.
   He or she is good with details.
   A prop designer, who is good with details, makes sure everything on a movie set
   looks realistic.

2. A screenwriter is a talented person. He or she develops a story idea into a
   movie script.
   A screenwriter is a talented person that develops a story idea into a movie script.

3. A script doctor is a writer. He or she is used when a screenplay needs
   more work.
   ....

4. Casting directors choose an actor for each part in a movie. They have
   usually been in the movie business for a long time.
   ....
   ....

5. High-budget movies always use big stars. The stars are known around
   the world.
   ....

6. Movie directors are greatly respected. They "make or break" a film.
   ....

Unit 15

1 Giving recommendations and opinions (page 101)

> ▶ *Ought to* has the same meaning as *should*, but it's more formal: Traffic signs **ought to** be obeyed. = Traffic signs **should** be obeyed.

A student committee is discussing rules for their school. Complete speaker B's sentences with appropriate passive modals. (More than one answer is possible.)

1. A: Students must be required to clean off the cafeteria tables after lunch.
   B: I disagree. Students .....*shouldn't be required*..... to do that. That's what the cafeteria workers are paid to do.
2. A: Teachers shouldn't be allowed to park in the student parking lot.
   B: Why not? Teachers .... to park wherever a space is available. After all, they're here for us.
3. A: A rule has to be made to ban the use of cell phones in school.
   B: I don't think a rule .... Students may need their phones for emergency purposes.
4. A: Students mustn't be permitted to use calculators during math exams.
   B: Sometimes we .... to use them, especially when we're being tested on more complicated concepts than simple arithmetic.
5. A: Something has got to be done to control the noise in the hallways.
   B: Students .... to talk to each other between classes, though. They aren't disturbing anyone when classes aren't in session.
6. A: Teachers must be required to remind students about important exams.
   B: That's unnecessary. On the contrary, students .... to follow the syllabus and check important dates on the course websites.

2 Tag questions for opinions (page 103)

> ▶ Tag questions added to statements in the simple present and simple past use the corresponding auxiliary verb in the tag: You **agree** with me, **don't** you? You **don't agree** with me, **do** you? You **paid** the rent, **didn't** you? You **didn't pay** the electric bill, **did** you?

Check (✓) the sentences if the tag questions are correct. If they're incorrect, write the correct tag questions.

1. Food is getting more and more expensive, ~~is it?~~ ....*isn't it*.........
2. Supermarkets should try to keep their prices down, shouldn't they? ....✓....................
3. People don't buy as many fresh fruits and vegetables as they used to, do we? ....
4. We have to buy healthy food for our children, don't we? ....
5. Many children go to school hungry, won't they? ....
6. Some people can't afford to eat meat every day, don't they? ....
7. We can easily live without eating meat every day, can we? ....
8. A lot of people are having a hard time making ends meet these days, haven't they? ....

Unit 16

1 Complex noun phrases containing gerunds (page 107)

> ▶ Complex noun phrases usually contain gerunds. Often they are also followed by gerunds: One of the most challenging things about **being** a teacher is **not becoming** impatient with difficult students.
>
> ▶ Different prepositions follow different nouns. Use *about* with *thing(s)*: What's the best thing **about** working from home? BUT Use *of* after *challenge(s), reward(s)* and *aspect(s)*: What's one of the rewards **of** being a social worker? One of the best aspects **of** being a social worker is helping people. NOTE: Use *of* or *about* with *part(s)*: What's the best part **about** being a mom? The best part **of** it is being a witness to your children's lives.

Read each situation. Use the words in parentheses to write a sentence with a noun phrase containing a gerund.

1. I work in an office. (one challenge = getting along with co-workers)
   One of the challenges of working in an office is getting along with your co-workers.

2. I have a job abroad. (most difficult thing = dealing with homesickness)
   ....

3. I work in a nursing home. (best aspect = helping people feel more positive about life)
   ....

4. I work in a rural clinic. (most frustrating part = not having enough supplies)
   ....

5. I'm a child-care worker. (one reward = making the children feel safe)
   ....

2 Accomplishments and goals (page 109)

> ▶ When talking about past accomplishments and including a specific time, use the simple past – not the present perfect: I **was** able to complete my degree last year. (NOT: I~~'ve been~~ able to complete my degree last year.)

A Complete the sentences about Ana's accomplishments. Use the verbs in parentheses. (More than one answer is possible.)

In the last five years, Ana . . .
1. *managed to finish* .... (finish) college.
2. .... (pay) all her college loans.
3. .... (start) her own company.
4. .... (move) to the city.
5. .... (make) some new friends.

B Complete the sentences about Ana's goals. Use the verbs in parentheses. (More than one answer is possible.)

Five years from now, Ana . . .
1. *would like to have expanded* ...... (expand) her business.
2. .... (meet) the man of her dreams.
3. .... (travel) to South America and Asia.
4. .... (get) married.
5. .... (buy) a house.

Grammar plus answer key

Unit 1

1 Relative pronouns

A: Ana, have you met Clint – the guy **X** Laurie is going to marry?

B: Oh, Clint and I have been friends for years. In fact, I'm the one **who/that** introduced Laurie and Clint.

A: Do you think they're right for each other?

B: Definitely. They're two people **who/that** have a lot in common – but not too much.

A: What does that mean?

B: Well, you don't want a partner **who/that** doesn't have his or her own interests. Couples **who/that** do everything together usually don't last very long.

A: I guess you're right, but the opposite isn't good, either. My last girlfriend was someone **X** I had nothing in common with. She wasn't the kind of girl **X** I could talk to easily.

B: Well, you can talk to *me* easily. . . .

2 *It* clauses + adverbial clauses with *when*

2. I hate it when I don't have enough time to study for an exam.
3. It doesn't bother me when friends talk to me about their problems.
4. It embarrasses me when I forget a co-worker's name.
5. I love it when my friends send me emails.
6. It upsets me when I have to wait for someone.

Unit 2

1 Gerund phrases

1. My brother's very interested in **becoming** a flight attendant. He dreams about **traveling** to new places.
2. I'm excited about **taking** a Japanese class next semester. I enjoy **learning** languages.
3. You wouldn't like **working** in a restaurant. You'd get tired of **standing** on your feet throughout the long shifts!
4. Our teacher is very good at **solving** problems. Maybe she should think about **changing** careers to become a guidance counselor.
5. **Making** a living as a photographer could be challenging. **Having** an impressive portfolio is really important to attract new clients and employers.

2 Comparisons

Answers may vary. Some possible answers:

2. A college professor earns more than an elementary school teacher.
3. Nurses have worse hours than psychiatrists.
4. Working as a police officer is as dangerous as being a firefighter.
5. A taxi driver isn't as well paid as an electrician.
6. Being a tour guide is less interesting than being an actor.

Unit 3

1 Requests with modals, *if* clauses, and gerunds

Answer may vary. Some possible answers:

2. A: Is it all right if I use your computer?
   B: You can use it, but please save my work first.
3. A: Would you mind giving me a ride to class?
   B: I'd be glad to. What time?
4. A: Can you help me move on Saturday?
   B: I'm sorry. I'm busy all weekend.
5. A: Would it be all right if I had another piece of pie?
   B: Yes, of course! Just pass me your plate.
6. A: Could you lend me your red sweater?
   B: Sorry. I don't like it when other people wear my clothes.

2 Indirect requests

2. Can you ask Susie if she wants to hang out with me?
3. Can you tell Susie to email me?
4. Can you ask Susie if she knows my address?
5. Could you tell Susie not to forget to write?
6. Can you ask Susie what she's doing on Saturday?
7. Could you ask Susie if she has any plans on Sunday?

Unit 4

1 Past continuous vs. simple past

1. A: How **did you break** your arm?
   B: It's a crazy story! Ramon and I **were riding** our bikes in the park when a cat **ran** out in front of me. I **was going** pretty fast, so when I **tried** to stop, I **went** off the road and **fell**.
   A: That's terrible! **Did you go** to the hospital after it **happened**?
   B: Yes. Luckily, we **weren't** too far from City Hospital, so we **went** there.
2. A: You'll never guess what **happened** to me this morning!
   B: What?
   A: Well, I **was brushing** my teeth when suddenly the water **went** off. I **had** toothpaste all over my mouth, and I couldn't wash it out.
   B: So what **did you do**?
   A: Fortunately, I **had** a big bottle of water in the refrigerator, so I **used** that water to rinse my mouth.

2 Past perfect

2. We had finished cleaning the house when our guests arrived.
3. Someone robbed my house yesterday because I had left the window open.
4. There was no food in the house because we had forgotten to stop at the supermarket.
5. I had called her three times when she finally answered.
6. I knew about the problem because your brother had told me about it.

Unit 5

1 Noun phrases containing relative clauses

2. a. Two things I'd be very interested in are the food and the music.
    b. The food and the music are two things I'd be very interested in.
3. a. Something I'd be worried about is not understanding the customs.
    b. Not understanding the customs is something I'd be worried about.
4. a. Two people I'd stay in touch with are my brother and sister.
    b. My brother and sister are two people I'd stay in touch with.
5. a. One thing I'd feel insecure about is speaking a new language.
    b. Speaking a new language is one thing I'd feel insecure about.

2 Expectations

2. When a friend sends you an email, you're expected to reply within a few days.
3. If you want to visit someone, it's not acceptable to show up without calling first.
4. If you invite a married couple to dinner, it's the custom for them to sit across from each other.
5. When you go to a birthday party, you're supposed to bring a gift.

Unit 6

1 Describing problems 1

1. A: Oh, no! These jeans **have a tear** in them.
    B: And they **are stained**, too.
2. A: This table has **some damage** on top.
    B: I know. The wood **is scratched** because my son drags his toy cars on it.
3. A: Why are you drinking out of that glass? It **has a chip** in it.
    B: Oh, I didn't see it. That's why it **is leaking**.
4. A: Someone hit my car today. Look! The door **has a dent** in it.
    B: I see that. Your back light **is broken**, too.
5. A: I bought this blouse yesterday, but I have to take it back. There **is a hole** in it.
    B: It's really cute, but that's not the only problem. It **has a stain** on it, too.

2 Describing problems 2

A

A: Look at this place! A lot of work **needs to be done** before we move in.
B: You're not kidding. Let's make a list. First, the walls **need painting**.
A: Right. And the windows **need to be washed**. Add the rug to your list: It really **needs to be cleaned**. Do you think it **needs to be dry-cleaned**?
B: No, I think we can do it ourselves. It **needs shampooing**. We can rent a machine for that.
A: And what about the ceiling fan? I think it **needs to be replaced**. Fans aren't too expensive.
B: OK. I've added it to the list. And what should we do with all this old furniture?
A: It **needs to be thrown out**! I think the landlord should take care of that, though.

B

I **keep having** technical problems. My computer **keeps crashing**, and my printer **keeps jamming**. I have to **keep putting** a new battery into my mouse because it **keeps dying**. The letters on my keyboard **keep sticking**, too. I **keep thinking** things will get better, but they just **keep getting** worse. Time for some new electronics!

Unit 7

1 Passive with prepositions

Answer may vary. Some possible answers:

2. Our soil is being contaminated due to the use of pesticides on fruits and vegetables.
3. Infectious diseases have been spread through improper disposal of medical waste.
4. Many different species are being endangered due to the destruction of their habitats.
5. Our air quality has been affected because of deforestation to make paper products.
6. Smog pollution has been reduced as a result of hybrid cars.

2 Infinitive clauses and phrases

A

2. b   3. d   4. c   5. a

B

B: Well, **one way to improve people's quality of life is to help them feel safe**.
A: That's right. **And the best way to do that is to create a larger police force**.
B: I agree. **Another way to make people happier is to make the air healthier**.
A: Yes. Good air quality is key. **The best ways to reduce air pollution are to ban cars and control industry**.
B: Maybe it's time to share our ideas with the mayor. Hand me my laptop.

Unit 8

1 *Would rather* and *would prefer*

1. B: I'd rather take classes at night.
2. A: Would you rather study business or education?
    B: I'd prefer to major in education.
3. A: Would you prefer to sign up for a biology course or an engineering course?
    B: I'd rather not take either.
4. A: Would you rather take computer science or history?
    B: I'd prefer not to take a class this semester.

2 *By* + gerund to describe how to do things

2. You can build your vocabulary by writing down new words and expressions.
3. Students can improve their listening skills by listening to English-language radio.
4. Hardworking students improve their grammar by not repeating common mistakes.
5. You can become fluent not by translating everything but by trying to think in English.
6. You can become a good conversationalist not just by talking with others but by talking when you're alone, too.

Unit 9

1 Get or have something done

2. A: Where can I get/have my computer repaired?
    B: You can get/have it repaired at Hackers Inc.
3. A: Where can I get/have my taxes prepared?
    B: You can get/have them prepared by my accountant.
4. A: Where can I get/have my hair cut?
    B: You can get/have it cut at Beauty Barn.
5. A: Where can I get/have my apartment painted?
    B: You can get/have it painted by Peter the Painter.

2 Making suggestions

A: I'm having trouble meeting people here in the city. Any ideas?
B: I know it's hard. Why don't you **join** a gym? That's usually a good place to meet people. Or maybe you could **take** a class at the community college.
A: What about **checking out** the personal ads? Do you think that's a good way to meet people?
B: I wouldn't recommend doing that. People never tell the truth in those ads. But it might be a good idea **to find** a sports team. Have you thought about **playing** a team sport – maybe baseball or volleyball?
A: I'm not very good at most sports, but I used to play tennis.
B: There you go! One option is **to look up** tennis clubs in the city and see which clubs have teams people can join.
A: Now, that's a great idea. And I could always use the exercise!

Unit 10

1 Referring to time in the past

A: Hey, Dad. Did you use to listen to the Beatles?
B: Of course. In fact, I just listened to one of their records a few days **ago**. Do you realize that the Beatles' music has influenced other musicians **for** over 50 years? They were the greatest!
A: Well, I just found some interesting information about them. I'll read it to you: "The Beatles were a well-known British band **during/in** the 1960s. They performed together **for** ten years – **from** 1960 **to** 1970. **In** 2003, the Beatles released another album, even though one of the original members had been dead **since** 1980 and another had died **in** 2001. The album had been recorded **in** 1969 and was in the studio safe **for** 34 years before it was released."
B: That is interesting. It's pretty amazing that people have listened to the Beatles **in** both the twentieth and the twenty-first centuries, isn't it?

2 Predicting the future with *will*

A: What do you think you **will be doing** five years from now?
B: I'm not sure. Maybe I **will have gotten** married by then. How about you?
A: I **will have finished** medical school, so I **will be doing** my internship five years from now.
B: So you **won't be living** around here in five years, I guess. Where do you think you **will live**?
A: Wherever I get my internship.

Unit 11

1 Time clauses

2. **Before** I got a full-time job, I had to live on a very limited budget.
3. **By the time** I finished high school, I had already taken three college courses.
4. **As soon as** I left for college, my mother turned my room into her office.
5. **Once** I left home, I realized how much my family meant to me.
6. **The moment** you have a child, you feel totally responsible for him or her.

2 Expressing regret and describing hypothetical situations

A

2. Ivan should have saved up for a car.
3. Jon shouldn't have been inactive when he was in college.
4. Lisa should have stayed in touch with her high school classmates.
5. Tony should have studied Spanish in school.

B

Answer may vary. Some possible answers:
2. If Ivan had saved up for a car, he wouldn't have to take public transportation.
3. If Jon hadn't been inactive when he was in college, he wouldn't have gained a lot of weight.
4. If Lisa had stayed in touch with her high school classmates, she wouldn't have very few friends.
5. If Tony had studied Spanish in school, he would be bilingual now.

Unit 12

1 Describing purpose

A

2. **In order to** stay popular, a website needs to be accurate and visually attractive.
3. **In order to** run a profitable furniture store, it's important to advertise on TV.
4. **In order for** a restaurant to stay in business, it needs to have "regulars" – customers that come often.
5. **In order to** establish a successful nail salon, it has to have a convenient location.
6. **In order for** an online business to survive, it's a good idea to have excellent pictures of the merchandise it's selling.

B

2. To stay popular, a website needs to be accurate and visually attractive.
3. To run a profitable furniture store, it's important to advertise on TV.
4. For a restaurant to stay in business, it needs to have "regulars" – customers that come often.
5. To establish a successful nail salon, it has to have a convenient location.
6. For an online business to survive, it's a good idea to have excellent pictures of the merchandise it's selling.

2 Giving reasons

A: I had to go downtown today **because** I needed to mail a package at the post office. **Since** I was only a few blocks from Main Street, I went over to Martin's. Did you know that Martin's has gone out of business? I'm so upset!

B: That's too bad, but I'm not surprised. A lot of family-owned shops are closing **because of** the construction of shopping malls.

A: Yeah, and don't forget about all the megastores that are popping up everywhere. **The reason why** people prefer to shop there is to save money. Everyone loves a megastore **due to** the low prices and the huge selection.

B: Not me! I loved Martin's **for** their beautiful clothes and friendly salespeople. When you were there, you almost felt like family. You'll never get that at a megastore!

Unit 13

1 Past modals for degrees of certainty

Answer may vary. Some possible answers:

2. A: What's wrong with Steven?
   B: Oh, you **must not have heard** the news. His dog ran away.

3. A: I went to see the Larsens today, but they didn't answer the door.
   B: Was their car there? If so, they **could have been** in the backyard.

4. A: Fabio said he was going to the party last night, but I didn't see him.
   B: Neither did I. He **couldn't have been** there then.

5. A: I can't find my glasses, but I know I had them at work today.
   B: You **might have left** them at the office.

6. A: Marc's new car looks really expensive.
   B: Yes, it does. It **must have cost** a fortune!

2 Past modals for judgments and suggestions

2. d   3. a   4. c   5. f   6. e

Unit 14

1 The passive to describe process

2. First, a business plan has to be written.
3. Next, market research should be done.
4. Then the competition needs to be identified.
5. Classified ads may be posted online.
6. Finally, employees are hired so the work can be started.

2 Defining and non-defining relative clauses

2. A screenwriter is a talented person who develops a story idea into a movie script.
3. A script doctor is a writer that is used when a screenplay needs more work.
4. Casting directors, who have usually been in the movie business for a long time, choose an actor for each part in a movie.
5. High-budget movies always use big stars that are known around the world.
6. Movie directors, who "make or break" a film, are greatly respected.

Unit 15

1 Giving recommendations and opinions

Answer may vary. Some possible answers:

2. A: Teachers shouldn't be allowed to park in the student parking lot.
   B: Why not? Teachers **should be allowed** to park wherever a space is available. After all, they're here for us.

3. A: A rule has to be made to ban the use of cell phones in school.
   B: I don't think a rule **has to be made**. Students may need their phones for emergency purposes.

4. A: Students mustn't be permitted to use calculators during math exams.
   B: Sometimes we **should be permitted** to use them, especially when we're being tested on more complicated concepts than simple arithmetic.

5. A: Something has got to be done to control the noise in the hallways.
   B: Students **should be allowed** to talk to each other between classes, though. They aren't disturbing anyone when classes aren't in session.

6. A: Teachers must be required to remind students about important exams.
   B: That's unnecessary. On the contrary, students **should be required** to follow the syllabus and check important dates on the course websites.

2 Tag questions for opinions

3. do they
4. ✓
5. don't they
6. can they
7. can't we
8. aren't they

Unit 16

1 Complex noun phrases containing gerunds

2. The most difficult thing about having a job abroad is dealing with homesickness.
3. The best aspect of working in a nursing home is helping people feel more positive about life.
4. The most frustrating part about/of working in a rural clinic is not having enough supplies.
5. One reward of being a child-care worker is making the children feel safe.

2 Accomplishments and goals

Answer may vary. Some possible answers:

A

2. has managed to pay
3. has been able to start
4. was able to move
5. managed to make

B

2. will have met
3. will have traveled
4. would like to have gotten
5. would like to have bought

Credits

Illustrations

Photos